IN FOCUS

CUBA

A Guide to the People, Politics and Culture

Emily Hatchwell
Simon Calder

The Latin America Bureau is an independent research and publishing organisation. It works to broaden public understanding of issues of human rights and social and economic justice in Latin America and the Caribbean.

First published in the UK in 1995 by Latin America Bureau (Research and Action) Ltd, 1 Amwell Street, London EC1R 1UL

A CIP catalogue record for this book is available from the British Library

ISBN 0 906156 95 5

Edited by: James Ferguson

Cover photograph by: Simon Calder

Cover design by: Andy Dark

Design by: Vincent Peters, Liz Morrell & Antonella Bianchi

Cartography by: Department of Geography, University College London

Printed by: South Sea International Press

Trade distribution in the UK by: Central Books, 99 Wallis Road, London E9 5LN

Distribution in North America by: Monthly Review Press, 122 West 27th Street, New York, NY 10001

Already published in the *In Focus* series:

Jamaica (1993)
Bolivia (1994)
Venezuela (1994)

CONTENTS

Vintage removals van, Havana

(Rolando Pujol/South American Pictures)

INTRODUCTION

Havana's Hilton Hotel must have seemed the height of fashion when it was built in the 1950s, with its 25 floors and lavish use of concrete. It was no accident that when Fidel Castro and his band of revolutionaries triumphed in January 1959, they chose the Hilton as their headquarters. They renamed the hotel the *Habana Libre*. Awash with young rebels in their fatigues, it became the symbol of Cuba's hope for freedom and a better future.

More than 35 years on, the hotel looks much the same, although its décor is now the epitome more of kitsch than of chic. Outside, American Buicks and Chevrolets splutter along streets lined by buildings untouched since before Castro and his men entered the city. In a typically Cuban anomaly, while time has seemingly stood still, life has also changed dramatically.

Fidel Castro put Cuba on the world map. He provided healthcare and education on a scale that his people had not dared to dream about. He helped to shake up a society rigidly segregated along class and racial lines. He was an inspiration to oppressed peoples and to socialists around the world.

The advances which have elevated the island above its partners in the developing world, however, have also raised Cubans' expectations and given them ambitions which their government can no longer satisfy. The economic crisis which struck the island following the collapse of communism in Europe, has presented the Revolution with its greatest challenge yet. After more than 35 years under the same leader, the country is grappling with the problem of adapting to a new and often harsh reality.

In the 1990s, the country's future is even harder to predict than it was in 1959. But despite the short-term uncertainties, compared with most Third World countries the prospects for Cuba's long-term future are good. Economically, the Caribbean's largest and most fertile island has great potential to be prosperous and stable. Furthermore, it has a huge North American market on its doorstep; whether Cuba wishes it or not, the US will almost certainly have as big an influence on its future growth as it has had on its economic decline.

Cuba has no parallel within the developing or the developed world, whether politically, economically or culturally. The Cuban national identity, a blend of chiefly Spanish and African influences mixed in a turbulent history of nationalism and revolution, is unique. This small country arouses extreme and polarised emotions, but never indifference. For most people who know Cuba, it is nothing less than an addiction.

Distinctive landscape of Viñales Valley,
with tobacco crop

(Rolando Pujol/South American Pictures)

1 HISTORY

– Before the Revolution

'one of the most rich and desirable possessions existing in the world'
General Leonard Wood, 1901

Cubans sometimes refer to their homeland as the 'sleeping alligator' because of its shape. The imaginary creature lies at the western end of the Antilles chain of Caribbean islands, close to the jaws of the Gulf of Mexico. Haiti is just 96km east and Key West, the southernmost point of the USA, 145km to the north. Cuba occupies about the same area as England but stretches over 1,200km from end to end. The capital, Havana, where more than two million of the island's population of eleven million live, sits on the north-western coast, near where the alligator's tail meets its body.

Cuba consists mainly of flat or gently rolling plains. The journey from Havana to Santiago de Cuba, the island's second city in the eastern half of the island (known as Oriente), involves an often monotonous drive through unrelenting sugar and citrus plantations. Europeans cross the Atlantic in order to lie on Cuba's beaches for two weeks, but the country's greatest natural asset are its mountains. There are three main ranges, the Cordillera de Guaniguanico in the west, the central Escambray mountains and the more rugged Sierra Maestra, which extends along the south-eastern coast and sheltered Fidel Castro and his fellow rebels during their campaign in the 1950s.

Thousands of islands pepper the waters around Cuba. Most of these show up merely as pinpricks on a map, but the Isla de la Juventud encompasses an area of about 2,330 square km. The island's post-revolutionary name, the Isle of Youth, given to it because many foreign students are educated there, evokes none of the mystery of the former Isle of Pines, on which Robert Louis Stevenson modelled his *Treasure Island*.

First Encounters Archaeology provides scant rewards in Cuba. The piecing-together of the island's early history relies much more on conjecture than on concrete evidence.

Tribes from Central or South America arrived in waves from around 1000BC, possibly even earlier. The Siboneys settled first, making their homes in caves and dependent on fishing. They survived only in the west of the island at the time of the Conquest, having been forced into a corner by the fiercer Taínos, a tribe of Arawak Indians who came from the Orinoco basin on the South American mainland, some as late as 1460.

The Taínos farmed and made pots, activities which represented the peak of sophistication in pre-Columbian Cuba. They enslaved the less-advanced Siboneys but were a peaceable tribe, ill-disposed to take much of a stand against the European *conquistadores*.

Christopher Columbus caught his first glimpse of Cuba on 27 October 1492 and declared that he had 'never seen anything so beautiful'. Convinced that he had reached the Asian continent of the Great Khan, he sent his men off in search of 'a king and great cities'. They found only small villages of thatched huts – the so-called *bohíos* on which Cuban peasants still model their homes – and people inhaling the smoke of 'certain herbs': this was the Europeans' first encounter with tobacco, one of the few legacies left by the Indians.

The Takeover   Spain showed little interest in Cuba at first. The occupation finally began in 1511, when Diego Velásquez disembarked with 300 men near Guantánamo Bay in the south-east. It was a swift and cruel affair which was wrapped up by 1514. The only real resistance was led by Hatuey, a fearsome Indian from the neighbouring island of Hispaniola, who tried to rally the Taínos by recounting tales of the Spanish atrocities from which he and others had fled. His reception was lukewarm, however, and he was eventually caught. Hatuey preferred death by fire to conversion to the Christianity of his captors.

The Spaniards were there only for easy spoils, and as soon as Cuba's gold ran out many of them headed off to the richer pastures of Mexico and Peru. Only geography prevented complete neglect of the island. Placed neatly at the mouth of the Gulf of Mexico, Cuba was crucial to the protection of Spain's waterways from attack by foreign fleets and pirates. The fledgling capital of Havana soon boasted Latin America's most formidable collection of fortresses and became the assembly point for Spanish ships heading back across the Atlantic.

Away from the hubbub of maritime activity in Havana, development was haphazard. The *encomienda* system, which gave the first colonisers a piece of land and a certain number of Indians to work it, was a feudal system infinitely worse than anything that existed in Spain. It forced the indigenous people into a life of slavery which in the end destroyed them; those who did not die of malnutrition, disease or maltreatment, killed themselves.

Slaves were shipped in from Africa to replace the depleted workforce. Many ended up on sugar plantations, where they were obliged to live like animals in huts called *barracones*. Slave-owners forced the strongest, healthiest men to breed with the fittest women to produce children whom they could then sell for a good price at auction. Rebellious slaves, known as *cimarrones*, fled their infernal lives and formed communities called *palenques*, mostly in the mountainous Oriente. Some blacks were able to buy their liberty, while others were released by masters undergoing deathbed repentances.

A Case of Monopoly The island's economy made only slow progress during the early colonial period, and until the 18th century, Cuba's claim to be 'The Pearl of the Antilles' stemmed largely from wishful thinking. It was foreign intervention which finally woke Cuba from its torpor.

Spain faced competition from other European powers in the Caribbean, and in 1762 the British finally managed to capture Havana. They returned the city to Spain in exchange for Florida after just eleven months, but during their short stay managed to change the course of Cuban history. By dropping the trade restrictions which had banned the island from doing business with any country other than Spain, the British opened up a new market for their merchants and helped to launch Cuba's export trade.

Back in Spanish hands, Cuba's economy received another unexpected boost in 1791, when a black revolution in the French-ruled half of Hispaniola, now Haiti, destroyed that territory's sugar industry. Almost overnight, Cuba took over the role as the largest producer of sugar in the Caribbean. The island's hardwood forests and grazing lands disappeared beneath a blanket of cane. In 1818, a royal decree opened Cuban ports to international trade and fuelled the sugar boom further.

The speed of economic development was matched by growing frustration among the creoles (*criollos*) – people of Spanish descent born on the island. Some of them had achieved considerable success as cattle-breeders and tobacco and sugar planters, but found their horizons curtailed by Spanish rule. The so-called *peninsulares*, born in Spain, formed an élite which not only controlled trade but was guaranteed the administration's top jobs, leaving the *criollos* with no say in the running of the country. The economic struggle gradually turned into a battle for political power, and ultimately for sovereignty.

¡Viva Cuba Libre! Many of the wealthiest *criollo* bourgeoisie favoured reform, but not necessarily a revolution. Greater than their desire for independence was their fear of blacks, a sentiment they shared with the *peninsulares* and one which developed into hysteria following the revolt in Haiti and the rapid rise in the number of slaves which accompanied Cuba's sugar boom; by the 1840s, slaves made up about 45 per cent of the population. Such fears were deep-seated enough to delay Cuba's bid for independence until

well after other Latin American countries (except Puerto Rico) had liberated themselves from Spain. Gradually, however, the impetus for independence passed to the *criollos* of Oriente. Left behind by the sugar boom in the west, small planters in Cuba's eastern province had little to lose by rebelling. Carlos Manuel de Céspedes launched Cuba's first war of liberation on 10 October 1868 by freeing his slaves.

Máximo Gómez, a defector from the Spanish army, and Antonio Maceo, a bold mulatto known as the 'Titan of Bronze', led a spirited campaign. They were eventually defeated not on the battlefield but by their *criollo* backers, who mistrusted the rebel army of peasants and blacks and capitulated to the Spanish in 1878. The Ten Years' War had killed more than 250,000 Cubans, including Céspedes, shattered illusions and destroyed the sugar industry. Nevertheless, it contributed to the abolition of slavery in 1886 and laid the ground for the next confrontation.

José Martí A short man with a long, melancholy moustache, José Martí was an unlikely leader of Cuba's independence struggle. Exiled to Spain in 1870 for his separatist views, he made his way to the US, where he wrote tirelessly and travelled around Cuban emigré communities to unite a revolutionary movement demoralised by defeat. Martí was the first man to define what the independence movement should be fighting for: not just self-rule but democracy and social justice. He advocated racial equality and rallied behind him both blacks, who had escaped slavery but not misery, and mixed-race mulattoes who faced systematic discrimination. They were joined by an increasingly class-conscious urban workforce and growing ranks of the frustrated middle class.

Martí believed that the Ten Years' War had been lost through bad organisation. He founded the Partido Revolucionario Cubano (PRC), the Cuban Revolutionary Party, to unify all those behind independence, and persuaded Maceo and Gómez to plan the new military strategy. The campaign began near Santiago on 24 February 1895. Facing a force five times its size, the liberation army pushed the enemy steadily westwards until by 1898, Spain and its commanders were exhausted militarily and economically. With the Cubans on the brink of triumph, the United States snatched victory.

How the War Was Won José Martí, shot dead in battle on 19 May 1895, had warned of North American expansionism. In a letter to a friend he had written, 'Once the United States is in Cuba, who will get it out?' The Americans had long coveted the island, and as early as 1807, Thomas Jefferson commented that Cuba would make a valuable addition to the United States. With an eye to a business opportunity, Americans had eagerly pursued Cuban planters

Cuban independence
fighters face Spanish
imperial troops in 1898

(Mary Evans Picture Library)

left impoverished after the Ten Years' War and bought up property at bargain prices. They soon dominated the sugar industry, and by 1895 more than 90 per cent of Cuba's sugar went to the US, along with the vast majority of its other exports.

Washington was reluctant to sacrifice such a profitable relationship for the sake of Cuban independence. Following the sinking in Havana harbour of an American ship, the *USS Maine*, in February 1898, Washington accused the Spanish of sabotage and declared war. (It was never proved that Spain was to blame.) Within months the colonial army surrendered to an American occupying force. The Treaty of Paris, signed on 10 December 1898, was negotiated behind the backs of the islanders and transferred sovereignty of Cuba to the US.

Washington contemplated annexation but in the end allowed the Cubans to elect their own government. There was much jubilation on 20 May 1902, as Cuba was declared a Republic and American troops began to withdraw. But the price paid for the end of military occupation was the acceptance of the Platt Amendment, which proclaimed Washington's right to intervene at any time 'for the preservation of Cuban independence'. It also provided for the establishment of the US naval station at Guantánamo Bay, 80km east of Santiago, to be leased 'in perpetuity'. The Amendment was repealed in 1934, but the naval base remained and has been a continual source of aggravation for Fidel Castro's government.

The Years of the Fat Cows

More than 300,000 people had died simply to replace rule by Spain with economic and political control by the US. Cuban history books describe the five decades which followed independence as the 'pseudo-republic'.

American monopolies cornered almost every sphere of activity. By 1925 they controlled electricity generation, owned the railways, while the Cuban Telephone Company did not even bother to give its network a Spanish name. But sugar held the key to American domination. By the 1920s, US companies produced more than half the annual crop. Small farmers were squeezed out by the large estates created to meet their northern neighbour's appetite for sugar. Other crops and industry were neglected, forcing Cuba to import everything from tomatoes to cars, supplied (most conveniently) by the US. Business bank accounts swelled while ordinary Cubans endured increasing poverty. Amid rising anger at the corruption of politicians, Gerardo Machado won the presidency in 1924 with his slogan 'honesty in government'. He started out well but later introduced Cuba to its first brutal military dictatorship. Social unrest intensified steadily until the labour movement, galvanised by the Communist Party, called a general strike in 1933. The show of popular discontent succeeded in toppling Machado and sparked a mini-revolution by an unlikely alliance of militant students from Havana University (a traditional hotbed of radical thought) and dissatisfied sergeants under a certain Fulgencio Batista. The army, however, had no intention of collaborating with the reformist government which emerged, and after three months Batista (by then a colonel) staged a coup.

The Rise of Batista

Batista enjoyed some initial popularity. A handsome mulatto of lower-class origins, he was a rarity among Cuba's ruling oligarchy, which was traditionally rich and white. The colonel manipulated a string of elections and presidents, but he also helped to implement one of the most progressive constitutions in Latin America. His flirtation with the Communist Party helped him to win the presidential elections in 1940, but he could not repeat the trick in 1944. Batista went into 'voluntary exile' while first Ramón Grau and then Carlos Prío were voted into the top job.

The Cuban people, disgusted by political corruption, oppression and their continued poverty, had begun rallying around Eduardo Chibás, leader of the Partido Ortodoxo or Orthodox Party. His calls for social justice made him a contender in the elections of 1952, but suffering from severe depression, Chibás shocked Cuba by shooting himself during a live radio broadcast on 5 August 1951. With his last words 'People of Cuba, rise and move forward! People of Cuba, awake!' etched in their memory, Cubans watched in horror as Batista returned from exile and, on 10 March 1952, staged a coup.

Fulgencio Batista imposed the harshest dictatorship Cuba had yet seen. He abolished the Constitution, dissolved Congress and crushed the opposition ruthlessly. Thousands died in the violence, but Washington supported him regardless.

Cuba enjoyed one of the highest per capita incomes in Latin America but wavered on the edge of social collapse. Misery reigned in the countryside while Havana glittered. The Cuban capital was one of Latin America's most sophisticated cities, and a byword for hedonism the world over.

The 'Fabulous Fifties'

Havana was *the* place to be seen in. A pantheon of America's rich and famous, from Marilyn Monroe to Errol Flynn, arrived by plane or aboard the *City of Havana* ferry from Key West. They glided around the Cuban capital in Cadillacs, which still cruise the streets in the 1990s, and entertained themselves drinking *daiquirís* and *mojitos* at Sloppy Joe's or the Floridita, Ernest Hemingway's favourite haunt. They splashed their money about the casinos or sought titillation from the sex shows at the Shanghai Theatre or from Havana's answer to the Folies Bergères, the Tropicana. Frank Sinatra was reputedly paid US$1,000 a night to perform at this, Latin America's most extravagant variety show. Graham Greene took Mr Wormold to it in *Our Man in Havana*: 'Chorus-girls paraded twenty feet up among the great palm-trees, while pink and mauve searchlights swept the floor. A man in bright blue evening clothes sang in Anglo-American about Paree.'

American gangsters swarmed to Havana. Batista and the Mafia controlled tourism between them, and they built many of the high-rise hotels, including the Hilton and the Capri, which still blight the city's skyline. The chief Mafiosi, the Lansky brothers, defended their patch as they did in New Jersey and Florida, although the murders never reached the scale seen on the mainland. After the Revolution, the Mafia fled and Cubans threw their roulette and fruit machines out onto the street.

From Moncada to Revolution On 26 July 1953, a young lawyer named Fidel Castro and 125 other militants attacked the Moncada barracks in Santiago de Cuba. The assault was as disastrous as it was daring, leaving most of the assailants dead. However, the 26-year old ringleader survived to stand trial and give the first great speech of his life. The speech became the basis for the political programme of Cuba's new revolutionary front, the Movimiento 26 de Julio or 26 of July Movement, named after the now sacred date of the Moncada assault.

Despite a sentence of 15 years in prison, popular pressure forced Batista to grant Fidel Castro and his fellow rebels an amnesty in May 1955. Forbidden from making public speeches, Castro left for Mexico City. A group of idealistic young revolutionaries gathered around him there, the most important new arrival being an Argentinian doctor called Ernesto 'Che' Guevara.

'It wasn't a disembarkation, it was a shipwreck' was Guevara's description of the landing of *Granma*, a leaking six-berth cabin cruiser which brought Castro and 81 revolutionaries from Mexico to Cuba in December 1956. The rebels lost almost all their equipment and only about 15 men, including Fidel's brother Raúl, made it to Pico Turquino in the Sierra Maestra mountains west of Santiago.

From such small beginnings, an extraordinary insurgency developed. The rebels spent the first six months winning over the peasants, whose collaboration Castro knew was vital to his cause. He predicted that promises of agrarian reform would win over the largely landless farmers and labourers, some of whom helped swell the ranks of the Rebel Army to between 2,000 and 4,000 (depending on which history book you read), compared with Batista's 50,000. Fidel Castro and his men expanded their operations throughout the Sierra, but they could not break out of the mountains. It was agitation in the cities, by the 26 of July Movement and other groups, which eventually drove Batista to end the military stalemate. In mid-1958 he launched his biggest attack ever against the rebels. It was a fiasco, and Castro responded by launching a counter-offensive in August, sending two columns westwards towards Havana.

With his armed forces rebellious, Batista fled to the Dominican Republic on 1 January 1959. A general strike called immediately afterwards showed overwhelming support for the rebels and the army surrendered. Fidel Castro made a triumphal procession across the island from Santiago, greeted along the way by thousands of ecstatic Cubans. He arrived in the capital on 8 January, but a more memorable date in 1959, New Year's Day, marks the anniversary of the Revolution's triumph – Liberation Day.

Fidel Castro

Fidel Castro Ruz, born in 1927 in Oriente, was the second of five illegitimate children born to a Galician plantation owner and his cook. His upbringing was strictly bourgeois; he attended a Catholic and then a Jesuit school, and in 1945 entered Havana University. Castro graduated in law in 1951 and married Mirta Díaz Balart, sister of a minister in Batista's government. But politics was the young man's passion. He tried conventional politics and joined the Orthodox Party, but after Batista's coup he decided that armed insurrection was the only option.

Fidel Castro, Raul Castro and Che Guevara, 1959   (Osvaldo Salas/Reportage)

Fidel Castro's success as a revolutionary leader has been due partly to his astonishing intellect and determination, but also to his charisma and ability to win affection: few citizens of the world are on first name terms, as are Cubans, with their leader. His personal influence has been decisive in guiding the people through the vicissitudes of the last 35 years.

Castro denies that he has encouraged a Stalinist cult of personality, and indeed statues and other images of *El Jefe Máximo* ('The Maximum Leader') are rare. His words, however, fill the newspapers and his voice is everywhere. Cubans have an enormous capacity to talk, but none more than Fidel Castro, who seems able to be eloquent about anything from the latest women's fashions to sewage treatment, and can speak for hours without a break. The years, however, have taken their toll; his speeches have grown progressively shorter from their fourteen-hour peak. And while he still has an awesome ability to arouse a crowd, the electric rhetoric is nowadays replaced increasingly by a tendency to ramble.

Fidel Castro envelops himself in a thick cocoon of protection, concealing his personal life. Rumours circulate about his womanising tendencies and numerous offspring. Officially he has two children, Fidelito and Alina, both of whom now live abroad, but there are almost certainly several more. After divorcing his wife in 1955, he has never remarried. Celia Sánchez, his assistant in the Sierra Maestra and later in Havana, was the closest companion Fidel Castro ever had. Since her death in 1980, the Cuban leader has appeared an increasingly lonely figure.

2 HISTORY OF THE REVOLUTION
– Island in the Storm

'History will absolve me'
Fidel Castro, 1953

Euphoria swept through Cuba in January 1959. The daring young revolutionaries became folk heroes overnight. Banners around Havana read 'Power to the Bearded Ones' (a reference to the rebels' hirsute appearance). Yet amid all the excitement Cubans began to wonder what lay in store. Fidel Castro had promised something to everyone, from agrarian reform to political democracy. Havana's bourgeoisie was unsure what to make of the middle class-turned-peasant soldiers with their aura of puritanical discipline. Some took fright and fled the island. Others seemed to think there would be a few reforms, free elections and then a return to business as usual. It soon became clear that Cuba was in for radical change.

But first there was retribution, for the murder of as many as 20,000 Cubans during the repressive campaigns of the 1950s. Calls for revenge rang louder than those for legal form. Revolutionary Tribunals, set up to deal with the so-called *Batistianos*, presided over show trials which sent most of the accused to the firing squad.

Taking Control

Soon after the *triunfo* (triumph), Fidel Castro and his rebels appointed Manuel Urrutia (a judge who had been sympathetic to their cause) as president, to head a government made up of representatives of the old political parties. But conflict quickly developed between the presidential palace and the *Habana Libre* Hotel, where Castro and his men were lodged in the early days, and where real authority lay. Urrutia was replaced by Osvaldo Dórticos, a more obedient figurehead president, while the old moderates were gently eased out in favour of *Fidelistas*.

The government passed more than 1,500 laws in its first year. Measures included pay increases and radically reduced rents. Most dramatically, the Agrarian Reform Law decreed *inter alia* that no farm could exceed 400 hectares, with anything above this going to the state. Within a year the government had acquired more than 40 per cent of Cuba's hitherto foreign-dominated farmland. Some of this was redistributed to landless peasants, but much of it was reorganised into state farms, providing secure jobs for labourers who had long suffered the so-called 'dead time' between harvests.

Revolutionary volunteer and peasant during literacy campaign of early 1960s

(Osvaldo Salas/Reportage)

Many of the early reforms put money in pockets overnight and won the government immediate popularity, but they did not stop speculation about elections. Castro, who had promised free elections from the Sierra Maestra, now declared that 'the Revolution has no time to waste in such foolishness'. The regime claimed that people showed their support by attending rallies, in a process dubbed 'direct democracy'. The government's confidence was not misplaced given its popularity at the time, but its suspension of the constitution and its refusal to seek a popular mandate provided extra ammunition for outside observers, above all in the US, who were increasingly alarmed at developments on the island.

Daggers Drawn   The US had maintained a fickle position during the war, initially supplying Batista with arms, later asking him to stand down and eventually recognising the new regime in Havana. Within weeks, however, it became apparent that Cuba and its neighbour were destined for confrontation.

Agrarian reform ruffled plenty of feathers in the US, but it was wholesale nationalisation which put an end to any chance of peaceful coexistence. During 1960, the Cuban government expropriated all American assets from oil refineries to the telephone network. By the end of the year there was almost nothing left. In a series of tit-for-tat measures, the Americans responded by reducing Havana's sugar quota and then, in October 1960, by

Cuban exiles captured during abortive
Bay of Pigs invasion, April 1961   (Hulton Deutsch)

cancelling sugar purchases completely and prohibiting all exports to Cuba except for food and medical supplies. Washington broke off diplomatic relations in January 1961, but President Eisenhower had already begun actively seeking to topple the regime.

Initially, the counter-revolutionary effort consisted of sabotage attacks in the cities and a small-scale insurgency in the Escambray mountains. But dependent on the assistance of the US Central Intelligence Agency, the guerrillas could not sustain a serious campaign. By late 1960 the Rebel Army had broken the counter-revolutionaries' resolve. In early 1961 the new man in the White House, John F. Kennedy, gave the go-ahead for an invasion, to be led by US-based exiles.

The Bay of Pigs

Political considerations aside, the Bay of Pigs attack was a shambles from its very inception. The idea that the people of Cuba would rise up against Castro following an invasion showed a complete lack of understanding of the situation on the island. Furthermore, everyone knew that Cuban exiles had been under CIA training since March 1960. Cuba was armed to the hilt by the time the invasion finally happened, with a huge militia force ready to defend the country.

American bombers utterly failed to destroy the Cuban airforce in advance of the land attack on 17 April 1961. This left Castro's pilots free to bomb US boats and planes, while an army of rebels and peasants dealt briskly with the enemy on the ground. The whole operation was defeated within just 48 hours. About 1,200 of the 1,500 exiles were captured and eventually exchanged for more than US$50 million worth of supplies from the US.

Kennedy was humiliated, Castro jubilant. David had beaten Goliath in what the Cuban leader called the 'first defeat of US imperialism in the Americas'. The incident gave a great boost to the Cubans. The CIA eased off its bomb attacks and concentrated instead on often ridiculous attempts to assassinate the Cuban leader, using everything from exploding cigars to cyanide capsules.

The Communist Cause

On 16 April 1961, the day after US planes bombed Cuban airfields in the prelude to the Bay of Pigs attack, Castro declared: 'They can't forgive our being right here under their noses, seeing how we have made a revolution, a socialist revolution right here under the very noses of the United States!' Two months later, communists were included in the ruling political alliance – from which the Partido Comunista de Cuba (PCC) or Cuban Communist Party was to spring in 1965. Amid universal speculation as to the political hue of the Cuban regime, news of Castro's shift towards communism reverberated around the world.

Fidel Castro had done nothing either before or after the triumph of the Revolution to dispel the mystery surrounding his ideological leanings. But on 2 December 1961, at the end of a tumultuous year, he explained to the nation, 'I am a Marxist-Leninist, and I shall be to the day I die.' Later, Castro said that he had hidden the fact that he was a Marxist in order to generate broader support for his revolution. But some Cuba-watchers view his emergence as a communist as evidence more of arch-pragmatism than political conviction, suggesting that it was part of his bid to prove his Marxist credentials to Moscow. With Cuba facing complete isolation by the US, the situation was simple: without Soviet support the Revolution would not survive.

Moscow had its doubts about supporting a revolution that was neither inspired nor imposed by the USSR. Furthermore, Cuba was on the other side of the world and not easy to control. Yet in the end, the prospect of having a client state in the Caribbean was irresistible. Hence, when the Cubans suddenly found themselves bereft of their American market, the USSR bailed them out. A delegation from Moscow agreed in February 1960 to an oil-for-sugar swap which helped sustain the Cuban economy through to the late 1980s. Trade with the other socialist countries also expanded rapidly. In 1959 Eastern Europe had been the destination for 2.2 per cent of Cuba's exports; by 1962 this was 82 per cent. Imports from the Eastern bloc rose from 0.3 per cent to 70 per cent.

Posters proclaiming 'Cuba is not alone' appeared in Havana. But it was a curious friendship. Cuba had far more in common with its enemy, North America, than with its new ally, the USSR. For its part, the Kremlin could not resist maximising political advantage from its new strategic position in the US 'backyard'.

The Missile Crisis Premier Khrushchev's statement in July 1960, that the USSR would defend Cuba against an American attack with its own missiles, had owed as much to bravado as to genuine enthusiasm for its role as protector. Yet when Havana requested military assistance in 1962, Moscow seized the opportunity to locate nuclear missiles within reach of its Cold War enemy.

More than 40 missiles had arrived by the time President Kennedy got wind of the affair. Outraged that the USSR was threatening the balance of power in the region, on 22 October 1962 he announced a strict embargo on the entry of offensive weapons to Cuba and demanded the withdrawal of missiles already on the island. Khrushchev refused. A Soviet convoy was heading towards Cuba. American ships were already in the area, while in the US nuclear weapons were prepared for launching. The world held its breath. After six long days, Khrushchev proposed that the Russians would withdraw their weapons if the US pledged not to invade Cuba. Kennedy agreed. The two superpowers had been teetering on the brink of nuclear war.

With the conclusion of the Cuban Missile Crisis, the stage was set for the duel which has persisted ever since. President Kennedy tightened up the trade embargo and declared, 'We will build a wall around Cuba.'

Domestic Opposition One reason that the Revolution succeeded in establishing itself comparatively easily was the emigration of half a million of the most disgruntled Cubans by the end of the 1960s. They were mostly members of the urban white middle class, and settled primarily in Miami. With much of the impetus for counter-revolution based abroad, a sustained challenge from within Cuba became impossible.

The neighbourhood Comités de Defensa de la Revolución (CDR), or Committees for the Defence of the Revolution, were founded early on to help the government ensure ideological conformity among the people. Anyone who was not with the Revolution was by definition against it. By 1965 an estimated 20,000 political prisoners were in Cuban jails and workcamps.

The Unidades Militares de Ayuda a la Producción (UMAP) or Military Units for Aid to Production represent one of the darkest moments of the Revolution. These labour camps were set up by the army in 1965 for the ideological rehabilitation of 'social deviants', a loose term which embraced anyone who was perceived as a threat to the Revolution, particularly homosexuals, dissident intellectuals and also Catholics.

The Revolution in Progress With immediate threats to the Revolution contained, greater attention could be directed towards economic development: a responsibility which was placed in the hands of Che Guevara, despite his inexperience in the field.

As Minister of Industry, Guevara oversaw the most radical phase of the Revolution. His programme was designed to overhaul not only the Cuban economy but also society as a whole. Fundamental to his plan for the redistribution of wealth was the rigid centralisation of the economy; by 1968 the government had nationalised all Cuba's private businesses, down to the last hot dog stand. The only exclusion was the permitted private farming sector. Far more controversial, however, was Guevara's idealistic vision of the *Hombre Nuevo* or 'New Man', the worker who replaces bourgeois ambitions of personal gain with elevated ideas of collective advancement. Cubans started working extra hours not for more pay, but for the honour of receiving praise in the local paper or a congratulatory banner.

Such measures could not counter the effects of the US embargo and the exodus of the country's most skilled professionals, nor make up for the new administration's lack of experience. The economy lurched from crisis to crisis. Agricultural production plummeted and rationing was introduced in 1962 (and has remained part of life in Cuba ever since). Guevara resigned in 1965 to go and do what he liked doing best, fighting guerrilla wars. Meanwhile, the regime ambitiously tried to mobilise hundreds of thousands of Cubans to reap a bumper 10-million ton sugar harvest in 1970 – and thereby solve the island's economic woes at a stroke. Not only did the attempt fail, but it also disrupted the whole economy in the process. With its economy in decline, Cuba headed deeper into the Soviet fold, a step dictated partly by Russian promises of substantial aid if Havana abandoned Guevara's Maoist programme in favour of a more orthodox communist line. Self-sufficiency had proved an impossible dream.

The early 1970s were hard and repressive years, but by 1975 the regime felt confident enough to stage the First Communist Party Congress. This launched a whole new political system of national and local government to spread decision-making away from Havana. But in reality the hegemony of the Party remained untouched by the new assemblies of *Poder Popular* or People's Power. A new constitution, approved by a referendum in 1976, recognised Marxism-Leninism as the state ideology and the Communist

Party as the only legal political organisation in the country. Fidel Castro's position as head of state became constitutional. Osvaldo Dórticos, puppet president since 1959, retired.

To Market If the 1975 Party Congress centralised political power, it also began a phase in which the government tried to loosen its grip on the economy, particularly in the field of agriculture. The goal of the communist regime had always been for the state to control the entire agricultural sector, and after the Revolution most sugar plantations were transformed into state farms. Cooperatives, where workers shared the profits, were also set up, but were dissolved almost immediately because neither Castro nor Guevara liked them. Even so, the private sector still accounted for about 30 per cent of agricultural land and proved to be far more productive than the state sector. Accordingly, cooperatives were revitalised after 1976, though the political goal of ultimate state control was not abandoned.

The economy had improved modestly by the end of the decade. Nonetheless, 1980 saw the most serious discontent against the Revolution since 1959 – an exodus in which 125,000 Cubans left for the US (see p.32). Clearly shocked by such a demonstration of dissatisfaction, Castro hurriedly sought to improve the quality of life in Cuba. In an attempt to boost food production, he introduced private agricultural markets, where farmers could sell any produce surplus to the quota they supplied to the state. These proved to be such a success that Cubans ate better than they had in years. But the government became convinced that it had created a class of *nouveau riche* speculators. Having also allowed limited self-employment in some trades, Castro was dismayed, too, by the verve with which Cubans abandoned state jobs in favour of the private sector. In 1986, he implemented the so-called Rectification of Errors, in which he dissolved the farmers' markets, reinstated hyper-centralisation and put the Party back at the heart of the national economy.

Life became much more difficult. While rations were reduced, defence spending rocketed; Ronald Reagan was in the White House and promoting an aggressive policy in the region. In the 1980s US regional policy led to the invasion of Grenada and sponsorship of the Contra civil war in Nicaragua. At the same time, Rectification was not having the desired effect, but so long as the USSR was willing to shore up the Cuban economy, the regime could weather the worst of the surrounding storms.

Exporting the Revolution

Cuba has been described as a small country with a large country's foreign policy, reflecting Castro's exalted idea of the island's position on the world stage. The Cuban leader gave new meaning to the word 'internationalism', a mixture of solidarity and pragmatism which became part of his strategy for survival. Supporting socialist causes abroad was largely an extension of Cuba's own Revolution.

Castro presented Cuba as a model for revolution around the world, and during the 1960s it was indeed an inspiration. He tried to encourage insurrection in Latin America, dreaming of turning the Andes into another Sierra Maestra. But Che Guevara's attempt to foment revolution among peasants in Bolivia failed miserably, and he was killed there in 1967.

At times it seemed that every Third World independence or liberation movement had called in the Cubans. Advisors and sometimes troops were despatched to numerous countries, especially in Africa. The biggest Cuban involvement was in Angola, where Havana supported the Marxist government in its struggle against rebels backed by the US and South Africa. More than 370,000 Cubans passed through Angola during the 15-year campaign which began in the 1970s. They managed some big successes on the battlefield, but in the face of a seemingly open-ended conflict, Castro settled for a negotiated agreement. The regime considers the 1988 accord to be a triumph, but although South African troops withdrew and Namibia was granted independence, Angola remains in a mess. Back home, people wonder whether the 2,077 Cuban casualties, most of whom perished through disease, died in vain in what some call 'Cuba's Vietnam'.

The Collapse of European Communism
In the USSR, President Gorbachev had been encouraging reform since the middle of the 1980s. While the Eastern bloc generally followed suit, Fidel Castro declared that Cuba would sink before it sacrificed socialism. The trial and execution of General Arnaldo Ochoa in July 1989 illustrated exactly what he thought of reform.

The truth behind the Ochoa case may never be known, but many Cubans believe that Fidel Castro built a case of corruption and failed drug-trafficking into a treason trial in order to take a potential rival off the scene. Not only was General Ochoa extremely popular among both ordinary Cubans and the soldiers who served under him, but he also advocated the sort of change which Castro could not tolerate; some had even talked of him as a possible successor. On his return from serving as Chief of Operations in Angola, Ochoa was destined to take charge of Cuba's western army. Castro almost certainly did not want a recalcitrant general in such a position of power.

Fidel Castro and Mikhail Gorbachev during   (Julio Etchart/Reportage)
Soviet leader's visit to Cuba, April 1989

Facing possibly the greatest political scandal in the history of the Revolution, after Ochoa's execution the Cuban leader launched an unprecedented purge of the ministries. By doing so he made it clear that he would brook no new thinking, within the military or elsewhere. Right-wingers among the increasingly vocal Cuban exiles in Miami claimed that Castro was losing his grip. Indeed, the odds were stacking up against him. The Berlin Wall had gone and politicians in Moscow mused about the logic of continuing any subsidy to Cuba. The island's fate was sealed in 1992 by the ascent to power of Boris Yeltsin, who was far more concerned about relations with Washington than with Havana. Any historical claim the island had to the USSR's affections became irrelevant once the union ceased to exist.

The Special Period

Since the Soviet bloc accounted for around 85 per cent of Cuba's trade, the social and political impact of its collapse was immediate and devastating. Confronted with its biggest economic crisis ever, the government in 1990 implemented the Special Period in Peacetime, an austerity package the likes of which Cubans had never seen.

The most significant shortage was of fuel. Since oil supplies from Eastern Europe (which had met 90 per cent of the island's needs) dried up, many factories and offices have ceased to function. A large proportion of the Cuban workforce has been left with nothing to do but count the *apagones*, the power cuts which still deprive Cubans of electricity for up to 16 hours a day. Public transport has ground almost to a halt. People travel crammed together in the back of the few trucks still on the road or by bike; the delivery of thousands of bicycles from China has caused the biggest transformation on the streets of Cuba since 1959.

The landscape in the countryside has turned medieval, as tractors have been replaced by oxen. With fuel for distribution unavailable, oranges and potatoes rot in the fields, while in the cities people queue instead for rations of imported rice and beans. For most Cubans, dairy products are a distant memory, and meat a luxury. In 1989, ration books could more or less guarantee a healthy diet. Within a couple of years this was no longer the case. Today, people generally look remarkably healthy and Cuba is free of the swollen stomachs and other tell-tale signs of malnutrition. However, vitamin deficiency was blamed for the outbreak of an eye disorder called 'optic neuritis' in 1993, which affected some 45,000 Cubans.

The US, determined to oust Castro, tightened its trade sanctions in 1992. The Cuba Democracy Act, introduced by Congressman Robert Torricelli, brought in a whole variety of restrictive measures, including the extension of the embargo to foreign subsidiaries of US companies. Pleas to exempt food and medical supplies were ignored. Discontent among Cubans spread, and the number of people trying to leave the island illegally by boat, bound for the US, grew steadily.

The Cost of Change

The embargo had started to bite long before the Torricelli Bill, and the Cuban leadership was forced to discuss solutions beyond simple belt-tightening. However, widespread anticipation that the Communist Party Congress of October 1991 would bring significant reform was dashed. The economy continued to shrink and by mid-1993 the government decided it had no alternative but to instigate liberalising policies.

Article 235 of the Penal Code, which states that anyone caught in possession of foreign currency may be imprisoned for up to five years, was the first casualty of the regime's new approach. Depenalising possession of the dollar (known colloquially as 'dollarisation') in August 1993 was designed both to harness the dollars circulating in the rampant black economy and to meet some demand for consumer goods unavailable for local *pesos*. Shortly afterwards, the government legalised small-scale private enterprise, bringing life to streets empty of small traders since the 1960s. These measures received a mixed reception among Cubans. Dollarisation was seen as being liberating but also socially divisive: most people with dollars were anti-Castro, involved in the black market or else had relatives in Miami; loyal revolutionaries, excluding party officials and other privileged citizens, tended not to have them.

The summer of 1993 saw an unprecedented spate of demonstrations in Havana. Castro responded by stepping up vigilance across the island and putting hundreds of suspected troublemakers behind bars. Tension increased steadily until it erupted once more in the summer of 1994. On 5 August 1994, there was a serious riot when police in Havana tried to prevent would-be refugees from boarding a ferry with the aim of sailing to Florida. Thirty-five police and civilians were injured in the worst unrest since the Revolution.

Blaming Washington for encouraging Cubans to flee in order to seek automatic political asylum in the US, Fidel Castro called off the coastguards, inviting an exodus. In a war of nerves, Cuban security forces stood by while refugees set off on makeshift rafts in the hope of being picked up at sea by US coastguard patrols: more than 30,000 were 'rescued' in a month. Within days, President Clinton was forced by domestic political pressures – and the impracticality of handling such a large influx – to reverse the US policy of granting automatic political asylum. The refugees were moved, ironically, back to Cuba to be held in camps at the naval base at Guantánamo.

Castro's astute strategy to pressure Washington into talking had worked. An agreement signed in New York provided for a more orderly exodus of Cubans, with the US agreeing to admit a minimum of 20,000 a year, compared with a previous average of nearer 3,000. But the basic problem remains: that many thousands of Cubans wish to leave a country they perceive as collapsing around them.

The events of 1994 may prove to have been simply another episode in an ongoing saga, but without doubt they helped to speed up the pace of economic reform. Private farmers' markets were allowed to open soon afterwards. Even so, Fidel Castro, the great survivor, seems intent on overseeing economic liberalisation without conceding significant political ground.

3   POLITICS

– Party and People

'To die for your country is to live'
Cuban National Anthem

Cuban society is the most politicised in the world. The Revolution which provides the people with cradle-to-grave healthcare, also provides cradle-to-grave politics. Cubans grow up well-versed in the achievements of their Revolution and the iniquities of their North American neighbour. Each morning, schools around the country echo with the sound of children chanting 'Pioneers for communism, we will be like Che!'

Party Politics

Cuba's daunting array of governing committees and councils, a soup of like-sounding names, conceals the simple fact that all political power lies in the hands of the Communist Party. Described in the Constitution as 'the highest guiding force of society and the State', the Party penetrates every sphere of activity on the island. No workplace is without its nucleus of members.

The Comité Central or Central Committee steers the Party, although an even tighter-knit group, the Buró Político (Politburo), sits at the pinnacle of power. Fidel Castro, as party leader, presides over the whole structure. Selected grassroots members have a chance to discuss policy at the congress held every five years, but in reality the big decisions are made beforehand by the leadership.

The assemblies of People's Power, created in 1976 to diffuse Havana's monopoly on decision-making, deal with the nuts and bolts of administering the country, but their political clout is negligible. The Asamblea Nacional, the 'supreme organ of state power', simply rubber-stamps Communist Party proposals into law. In recent years the televised debates in the National Assembly have provided better watching than in the past, but the show of obedient hands during voting illustrates the limits of Cuban democracy and the reluctance to gainsay the leadership. The vast majority of National Assembly delegates are Party members and the big names in the Central Committee also dominate Cuba's top government bodies – the Consejo de Ministros and the Consejo de Estado. The first, the Council of Ministers, is the highest ranking executive and administrative organ. The Council of State represents the National Assembly between its brief twice-yearly sessions and is authorised to issue decrees. Its president – a post invariably belonging to Fidel Castro – is automatically both head of state and head of the government, and also proposes members of the Council of Ministers for election by the National Assembly. Fidel Castro's full title is: Commander-in-Chief, First Secretary of the Central Committee of the Cuban Communist Party and President of the Councils of State and Ministers: *El Presidente* for short, although the official title 'President of the Republic' no longer exists.

In 1993, Cubans for the first time elected deputies to the National Assembly in a direct ballot. This was certainly a breakthrough for Cuban democracy, but the people still voted for a single list of officially-approved candidates. Castro has not noticeably changed his view of Western-style democracy, which he described as 'complete garbage' during the 1991 Party Congress. He insists that the Cuban system is 'incomparably more democratic than any other.'

Mass Organisations

The Communist Party is an élite club, made up of the country's top workers and professionals, including those careerists who see Party membership as a vehicle towards the peak of their profession. The work of rallying Cubans around its ideological agenda is handed to the mass organisations, which are not officially controlled by the Party but are inextricably linked to it. They cater to the interests of each sector of society, from women to farmers, but they exist more to ensure that every citizen makes his or her contribution towards the construction of socialism than to express their members' particular aspirations. The Central de Trabajadores de Cuba (CTC), the central trade union organisation, works hard to maintain production levels, but unionists were stripped of their right to strike long ago. The Unión de Jovenes Comunistas (UJC), the Union of Young Communists, with its umbrella youth groups, is there to instil revolutionary spirit in students rather than to campaign for more school books.

As well as rounding up volunteers to help with the sugar harvest or bussing people off to attend a rally, the mass organisations are responsible for involving Cubans actively in the defence of the Revolution. At weekends, people of all ages troop off to practise emergency drills, dig trenches or build barricades. The people's militias now make up a force of 1.3 million, although the leadership claims that Cuba has over six million people trained and organised to defend the country. The armed forces, army reserves and state security troops account for approaching 450,000 of these, but the rest are ordinary people.

The Men in Green

The regime which is said to have contemplated abolishing the army after the Revolution now boasts one of Latin America's largest armed forces. The presence of an aggressive neighbour to the north provided reason enough for Cuba to build up its military might. Drumming up hostility against the US and playing on traditional nationalist passion for the *patria* or homeland have been central to the militarisation of the Cuban people. From an early age Cubans learn to regard the guerrillas who fought in the Sierra Maestra as epitomes of revolutionary virtue. Even so, many young men feel only loathing for the compulsory military service, on which the regime relies for almost half of its 180,000 regular troops.

The financial crisis has forced huge reductions in Cuba's military capability; symbolically, on 1 May 1993, the traditional parade through Revolution Square consisted of soldiers riding past on bicycles rather than the usual exhibition of military hardware. Cuts have been offset to some extent by improved efficiency, but the task of maintaining the morale of the armed forces, Castro's ultimate guarantee of power, falls on Raúl Castro – a rather puny figure alongside his brother Fidel, but in reality a tireless military leader. The siblings together personify the intimate link between the armed forces and political power. The vast majority of army officials belong to the Party, and a quarter of the 25 members of the Politburo wear uniform.

Dealing With Dissent

There are no death squads in Cuba and there is no evidence of systematic torture. Castro's regime seems mild in comparison with some of Latin America's recent dictatorships. What exisis in Cuba is a more sophisticated ideological suppression, justified politically as the subordination of the rights of the individual to those of society as a whole. The official line is that personal sacrifices are essential if Cuba is to preserve the system which supplies such benefits as free healthcare and education, considered by the regime to be fundamental human rights.

Yet is the loss of personal freedom in exchange for more doctors and more schools a justifiable sacrifice in the defence of Cuban socialism? Cubans who challenge the parameters of freedom imposed by the regime presumably do not think so.

While only the very best workers can hope to be accepted into the Communist Party, anyone may join a mass organisation. Only by doing so can they prove their revolutionary credentials. Cubans who refuse to 'integrate' politically find their chosen career barred to them or promotion refused. The price paid for political indifference, let alone dissent, is a black mark on their dossier, which may be consulted when they apply for a new job or if they get into trouble with the authorities.

The weight of the law bears down more heavily on those guilty of active political dissent. The most common charge used to imprison someone who expresses opposition is of disseminating 'enemy propaganda', which can include anything from talking to a foreign journalist to distributing subversive leaflets, and carries a sentence of up to eight years.

Repression eased somewhat in the 1980s, but in response to the instability which followed the break-up of the USSR, the regime has hardened its response to perceived dissidents. Over the last few years thousands have been imprisoned under the charge of *peligrosidad* or 'dangerousness', a concept used to punish 'anti-social' behaviour, and which targets anyone who threatens the social or political order. The charge has proved ideal for removing disaffected youth and other potential trouble-makers from circulation – particularly black marketeers, viewed not just as a threat to the national economy but also as liable to corrupt others. In a system of justice censured by Amnesty International, court hearings last a matter of minutes and usually result in a sentence of one to four years in an agricultural work camp.

The Security Apparatus

Cuba is a police state. The regime justifies high levels of security by pointing to threats – internal and external – to the Revolution. Its critics accuse it of systematically repressing its citizens. The Ministry of the Interior (MININT) is in charge of preserving law and order and deploys all-in-blue police by the thousand. Its Departamento de Seguridad del Estado, the KGB-style Department of State Security, deals with dissidents. Harassment by both groups, including short-term arrests without charge, has risen in tandem with worsening economic conditions.

The work of the security forces would be a lot harder without the involvement of ordinary Cubans. The Committees for the Defence of the Revolution engage in community projects such as vaccination campaigns, but their main job is to act as the government's civilian spy network; each CDR – there is one on every block – keeps files on the personal life of the local inhabitants. The Brigadas de Respuesta Rápida, formed in 1991, are nothing short of organised mobs, which intimidate dissidents by laying siege to their homes, chanting slogans and sometimes beating them up. These Rapid Response Brigades usually include members of the security forces, but still show the passion with which some civilian Cubans are willing to defend the Revolution.

Dissident Organisations

Fidel Castro insists that the vast majority of Cubans remain loyal to the regime. In reality, it is hard to say how much support it has. Some Cubans hide their feelings beneath a veneer of revolutionary loyalty. Others show discontent by referring to the President as 'Castro' rather than the traditional and affectionate 'Fidel', or, more boldly, as the 'Barbarian' or 'Red Devil'. But few Cubans take the step of joining what opposition organisations exist. Many are either bored by politics or are too busy simply surviving. Emigration (legal or illegal) has always been the most effective gesture of disapproval.

The assiduous work of the CDRs and security forces keeps clandestine political activity down to a minimum. However, the recent trend for forging coalitions (with titles even more confusing than those of Cuba's governing bodies) has increased the impact of the fifty-odd small and scattered opposition groups. Castro describes all of them as mere putty in the hands of right-wing Miami exiles, but most are increasingly reasonable in their demands for peaceful dialogue and democratic elections. There are 'revolutionaries' among them too, who support the aims of the 1959 Revolution – but not what it has become.

The Corriente Socialista Democrática (CSD) poses perhaps the greatest threat to the government because it is willing to contemplate reform with Castro still in place and attracts disenchanted communists. Elizardo Sánchez, one of the Democratic Socialist Current's founders, is Cuba's most famous dissident but has been attacked by both communists and anti-Castroists for his message of reconciliation. The other main alliance is the centre-left Concertación Democrática Cubana (CDC), the Cuban Democratic Convergence, which includes Criterio Alternativo, a small party of intellectuals led by María Elena Cruz Varela, whose poems have earned her both prizes and a prison sentence.

The number of political prisoners in Cuban jails remains one of the government's best kept secrets; a dearth of information (plus disagreement of what constitutes a 'political' prisoner) renders most estimates either extremely conservative (500) or wildly exaggerated (50,000). The regime's cooperation with UN human rights observers has been patchy, largely because Havana believes UN reports to be heavily US-influenced and thus politically motivated.

US-Cuban Relations Wayne Smith, former head of the US diplomatic mission in Havana, once said that Cuba has the same effect in Washington that the full moon has on werewolves: rational behaviour ceases at the mere mention of the place. Fidel Castro reserves his most strident language for attacking the US, but most people find it easier to comprehend his anger than to understand Washington's obsession with crushing the small nation that dangles from its southern shore.

Mariel The Cuban leader has so far succeeded in foxing nine US presidents, including those who started out with good intentions. President Jimmy Carter opened talks with Havana in the late 1970s and even established limited diplomatic relations. But the Mariel boatlift in 1980 left him looking as foolish as Kennedy did after the Bay of Pigs invasion.

In April 1980, twelve dissidents forced their way into the Peruvian embassy in Havana to seek asylum. More than 10,000 Cubans followed. Probably relishing Castro's discomfort amid such a crisis, President Carter declared that the US would welcome political refugees with 'an open heart and open arms'. Castro, said to be enraged by the remark, replied by opening the port of Mariel near Havana and permitting an exodus. The number of Cubans wishing to leave may have embarassed the regime, but always a master at turning a crisis to his advantage, Castro used the boatlift to get rid of several thousand criminals, mental patients and other 'undesirables'. It was Carter who eventually called a halt to the five-month flood in which 125,000 Cubans left.

Revolutionaries dubbed the defectors *escoria* or 'scum'; they were barely more popular in the US. The largely middle-class exile community in Miami disliked the social make-up of the so-called *Marielitos*, on whom they still blame their city's crime problem.

Cubans in Exile

Cuban emigré communities exist from Spain to Costa Rica, but the majority of exiles have settled in Florida. It is tempting to regard the one million-plus Cubans who live in Miami as a homogenous mass, but there are many layers to the community. That the exiles have such a right-wing image is thanks to the landowners and businessmen who were the first to flee after the Revolution and have since amassed large fortunes. The Cuban-American National Foundation (CANF), the most high-profile right-wing group, not only supports the embargo but favours a full-blown blockade, and will clearly not be satisfied until Castro has been forced from office. CANF has managed to acquire enormous clout in Washington – so much so that its chairman, Jorge Mas Canosa, stood alongside President Bush at the signing of the Torricelli Bill in 1992. Canosa does nothing to hide his ambition to be president of Cuba one day. He has already drawn up his economic strategy for a post-Castro Cuba, which envisages the island as a free enterprise semi-client state along the lines of Puerto Rico.

While most Miami exiles want to see the back of Castro, not all of them are motivated by financial or political ambitions. The majority are concerned above all about the well-being of families and friends in Cuba; and some, however much they dislike Castro, even see the wisdom of negotiating with the regime.

Polls generally suggest that 20-30 per cent of exiles, mostly the older generation, would return to a post-Castro Cuba. It is difficult to see how they would adapt easily to life in a country very different from the one

Cuban rafters await rescue by US coastguard, 1994   (C Brown/Saba-Rea)

Dire Straits

Fidel Castro's daughter, Alina, escaped to Atlanta in 1993 disguised as a Spanish tourist. Airforce pilot, Orestes Lorenzo, flew to Key West in his own plane in 1991, returned the following year to pick up his family and then wrote a book about it. For most Cubans, escape means a more mundane but treacherous journey by sea north across the Florida Straits. Only the bravest or most desperate risk putting themselves at the mercy of sharks and the rough seas; people reckon that as many as 50 per cent of *balseros* or 'rafters' never make it. The average raft consists of one or two lorry inner tubes stabilised by wooden planks and polystyrene blocks, a flimsy construction which can be sunk or shattered by a single heavy wave.

they left. In Cuba itself, there is a real fear that should Castro's regime fall, the island could be swamped by US and Cuban-American interests. Blacks in particular dread domination by the mainly white exiles; and some Cubans worry, with justification, that they will be forced out of their homes by pre-1959 owners. The only thing most Cubans would accept from the Americans is their money. Not even Fidel Castro himself would reject the exiles' financial help, and he has already held discussions with moderate exiles regarding investment opportunities in the island.

Room for
Manoeuvre? The events of August 1994 – when Castro called off the coastguards and allowed anyone who could put together a raft to leave – was typical of the relationship between Cuba and the US, in which Havana has called the shots and Washington has merely reacted.

More than any of his predecessors, Bill Clinton has had to battle with the contradictions inherent in White House policy towards the island. With the Cold War over, the US restored ties with China and Vietnam, and is talking to arch-communist North Korea. Yet Washington refuses to compromise over Cuba, even though the embargo has proved effective only in deepening the misery of the Cuban people and providing Castro with a convincing excuse for his country's problems. Vindictive US policy ensures too that the Cuban leader can continue to count on a sizeable body of support among a fiercely patriotic population.

Many US citizens are rapidly losing patience with their government's blinkered approach to Cuba; a poll in 1994 showed that 51 per cent believed the embargo should be lifted, and people have already started to defy the Trading with the Enemy Act, which bans Americans from travelling to the island. Nevertheless, the new Republican Congress began moves early in 1995 to tighten the embargo, including sanctions against foreign companies investing in Cuba. US entrepreneurs watch gloomily as competitors from Europe and elsewhere move into the Cuban market, while politicians begin to question why millions of dollars of taxpayers' money are spent financing TV Martí, a propaganda channel broadcast from Miami which no one in Cuba can tune into.

The White House would not deny that the embargo is designed to spark economic misery and ultimately social unrest in Cuba, but the exodus of 1994 should have shown the US government that instability in the island is the last thing it needs. Furthermore, there is virtually no support for the embargo abroad: in 1994, 101 countries in the UN General Assembly voted against the embargo, compared with just two in favour.

White House policy towards Cuba is dictated largely by domestic concerns and by election hopes in particular. Going soft on Cuba wins no votes among the traditionally Republican exiles in Miami – from whom both political parties receive substantial campaign funds. Any prospect that relations between Washington and Havana might improve was destroyed by Republican gains in the 1994 congressional elections. And so far, Bill Clinton has lacked the political nerve to push for an end to a battle which most people feel has gone on far too long.

The World View

Of all the guests at Nelson Mandela's inauguration as South Africa's President in 1994, Fidel Castro received the most rapturous welcome. The mystique of the Cuban Revolution, which abroad has not been dulled by the grind of hardship, still arouses genuine affection for its leader. *Granma*, Cuba's Communist Party paper, prints daily messages of solidarity from around the world: gestures of support for the defiant stand by a small nation against the world's only superpower.

The world view of Castro's regime has always been dominated by the US. After Cuba was thrown out of the Organisation of American States in 1964, owing to pressure from Washington, all member states broke off diplomatic relations – except for Mexico, which has proved to be one of Castro's most faithful allies. Gradually bonds with other countries have been repaired. Latin American nations have become increasingly vocal in their opposition to the embargo.

Even when he was most dependent on subsidies from the USSR, Castro was a leading light in the Non-Aligned Movement. He has also nurtured some dubious alliances with nations shunned by the rest of the world, including the regime of Saddam Hussein during the Gulf War. But despite some questionable diplomatic policy-making, Cuba has retained a strong solidarity network overseas. Humanitarian aid has poured in, with substantial donations from Spain, Germany, Canada and even organisations in the US. For years, brigades of volunteers have flown in to assist with coffee and other harvests.

Parody

Whither Cuba?

In 1993, Castro declared that 'capitalism is a failure which offers no future whatsoever to humanity.' In a painful ideological contortion, he hopes at the same time to use capitalist measures to save Cuban socialism. His concessions towards market economics have been dubbed *capitalismo frío*, 'cold capitalism'.

Fidel Castro does not hide the fact that the government has whittled away at the communist economic system purely through necessity. But how much can he give into capitalism without sacrificing socialist society and, more importantly, without losing control of his country? As loudly as Castro calls for the lifting of the embargo, he knows that liberalising trade between Cuba and the US could herald the end not only of his regime but of Cuban socialism. Washington argues that calling off the embargo unilaterally could give a new lease of life to Castro, but it is unlikely that he would be able to control the impact of a flood of North American money, people and ideals. Foreign investment so far has not been so heavy as to undermine seriously the Cuban political system.

Dilution of his ideology

Reform From Within?

The prediction of Castro's demise has been a favourite pastime ever since the Berlin Wall fell in 1989. The Cuban leader has proved adept both at outliving his political obituaries and at tantalising speculators about his future. His declaration in early 1994 that 'revolutionaries do not retire', was followed some months later by a statement saying that if the Americans lifted the embargo he would resign. While it would seem out of character for Castro to stand down, it also seems highly unlikely that he would oversee the kind of democratic reforms which he himself has said will eventually come to Cuba. His speeches which, like the billboards in the streets, are still designed to extract political advantage from the heroism of the Revolution, seem of scant relevance to the island's current struggle. Yet with his country in a state of collapse, more than ever in the history of the Revolution, Fidel Castro is the glue which binds Cuba together.

Reform from within the government, with Castro still in place, will provide the country with the best chance of a peaceful move towards democracy. Without the *Jefe Máximo*, the Party would almost certainly split into factions, provoking a battle between the new and old thinkers. In such a situation, the role of the armed forces could be decisive. The army appears to show no tendency to mutiny, but without Castro in power, no one can say which way its political allegiance would swing.

The younger generation within the Party has for some years been trying to engineer a peaceful succession, aware that the leader's sudden disappearance from the scene would result in chaos. In the run-up to the 1991 Party Congress, the Politburo discussed a 'dream succession', in which Fidel Castro would remain as president and head of the Party, but a younger prime minister would be appointed to run day-to-day affairs. But the reformist wing failed to allay the old guard's fears that liberalisation could spin out of control and destroy the Revolution.

The problem about discussing who might take over from Fidel Castro's is that he does not have an obvious successor. In the past, people presumed power would default dynastically to Raúl Castro. The President's brother and deputy has shown himself to be increasingly receptive to economic reform, giving rise to speculation that he is trying to bolster his position (and that of the army) in the event of political turmoil. But he still has a reputation for being a hardliner and is not popular among Cubans. Judging from the way younger politicians have been promoted into the upper echelons of power, Fidel Castro would prefer to hand over to the next generation. All the newer faces in the Party have so far remained fiercely loyal to their leader, but they also see a pressing need to adapt to a new reality.

Foremost among the possible contenders is Roberto Robaina, who became Foreign Minister in 1993, aged just 37; giving such an important job to one so young and inexperienced was interpreted as Castro's endorsement of his future successor. The most powerful alternative to Robaina is Carlos Lage, Minister of Economic Planning, whom ordinary Cubans appear to favour. The third main challenger is Ricardo Alarcón, the sharp-tongued president of the National Assembly, who is in his late 50s but has far greater experience than his younger colleagues and has shown himself to be a skilful negotiator abroad.

Castro or Chaos

'And if, in order to crush the revolution, they have to kill all the people, the people, behind its leaders and its Party, will be willing to die!' The kind of faithful revolutionaries who energise the rallies over which Fidel Castro presides, would probably not hesitate to defend their country to the end. But the desperation with which Cubans fled in 1994 suggested how many people would also rather die leaving by raft than fighting to defend the system.

Many would also rather leave than fight against the system. There is no great stomach for rebellion in Cuba. Many fear that a popular uprising would lead to bloody civil strife as years of frustration and hatred would explode and pitch Cubans against one another. And what would the alternative be? Chaos seems a more realistic prospect than liberal democracy, a political system Cubans have never known.

A mixture of patriotism, distrust of the Miami emigrés and sheer resilience may partly explain the Revolution's survival. However bad things are now, the old revolutionaries say, they were infinitely worse under Batista. But more than half of all Cubans have been born since the Revolution and take education and healthcare for granted. They are bored by the system and the unchanging face of the leadership, and are hungry for consumer goods and a chance to live their lives to the full. The future of Cuba lies in their hands.

4   ECONOMY

– State and Market

'We are now trying to navigate through an economic Bermuda Triangle.'
Gerardo Trueba, Cuban government economist, 1993

Cuba's resources suggest that it should easily be the strongest economy in the Caribbean. Agricultural potential is strong; its mineral wealth is significant; and its share of the world's biggest industry, tourism, should be the largest of any Caribbean island. Furthermore, the labour force is every investor's dream: young, healthy and highly educated. But in five years from 1988, *per capita* GDP had fallen from around US$2,000 to less than half that figure, with widespread shortages and a virtually worthless *peso*.

So what went wrong? At a time when virtually every other nation in the world (some with strong ideological reluctance) was moving towards free-market reform, Fidel Castro refused to permit private enterprise. For years, he could afford to preside over a grossly inefficient economy because of the enormous subsidy provided by the USSR. But since 1990 the island has teetered on the edge of an abyss. The embargo has been held responsible for the near-collapse of Cuba's economy, but in reality the US has simply twisted a knife which was already deeply embedded. Ironically, the fact that the country continues to function at all is due in large part to the remittances sent by Cuban exiles in the US to relatives on the island, and which are said to be worth over US$300 million a year. Although Washington put a stop to these payments after the exodus in 1994, money still filters through in substantial quantities.

A Tale of Two Super-powers
Prior to 1959, Cuba was effectively owned and operated as a subsidiary of the US. Investment in everything from sugar to illegal sex originated in North America. The economy generally performed well, especially in the boom years of the Eisenhower presidency, but always in an extraordinarily iniquitous fashion. The workforce was exploited, profits repatriated and the island's infrastructure engineered for the benefit of foreign interests. Anger at this economic colonisation was one reason why the Revolution's expropriation of North American assets, received such popular backing. Not in Washington, however, which still claims that Cuba nationalised some US$8 billion worth of US-owned property without adequate compensation.

The Cold War enabled the revolutionaries to get by without their northern neighbour. The political shift, first to socialism then to communism, mirrored the economic move into the Soviet sphere of influence. By joining an economic world which was independent of the US, Cuba could wriggle free of the constraints imposed by the embargo. When, in 1976, Cuba joined COMECON (the communist common market), it plugged into a system where it could make a unique contribution. East Germany got fresh fruit, Czechoslovaks could take Caribbean holidays and Soviet citizens from Vilnius to Vladivostok enjoyed Cuban sugar.

Sugar-cane was at the root of the deal with the USSR. Moscow guaranteed Cuba a price for its harvest. Not only was this usually well above the world price, but it also gave the economy a degree of stability unknown to the rest of the commodity-dependent Caribbean. Payment was made in oil at a price both predictable and well below the going rate, and Cuba was free to sell the surplus on the world market. Thanks to this deal worth US\$5 billion a year, Cuba could fuel its development and feed, educate and treat its people. Bread made from Soviet wheat formed part of Cubans' daily diet, and consumer goods were widely available, even if they were of poor quality.

The Economic Roller-Coaster

The idea that Cuba's economy started to go wrong only after 1989 is an illusion. The inability of such a fertile tropical island to feed its population, for example, results not only from the pressure to export as much as possible to earn hard currency, but also from a serious mishandling of the economy. This stemmed in particular from the penchant for hyper-centralisation and from economic management based more on improvisation than long-term planning. This state of affairs did not really matter as long as the USSR could make up the shortfall: before communism collapsed, more than 70 per cent of Cuba's foreign trade was with the USSR, and another 15 per cent with the rest of the Eastern bloc.

At the January 1990 COMECON meeting, it was recognised that economic ties between Moscow and Havana would continue, but that transactions were to be made in hard currency. The USSR massively reduced its levels of support to Cuba and GDP plummeted. Structural reforms began at last in 1992. Institutions were forced to justify themselves economically as the steady supply of cash from the central planning authorities gradually dried up. Ministries were obliged to seek their own ways of earning hard currency; even the armed forces and the Union of Young Communists have dabbled in tourism.

In July 1993, Castro announced that Cuba's imports had fallen from over US\$8 billion in 1989 to a mere US\$2.2 billion in 1992. Drastic action had to be taken. The government began streamlining state firms, eliminating some and merging others. The subsidies which had cushioned Cubans, and

Shop window in Havana
(Emily Hatchwell)

kept prices at levels almost unchanged since the 1960s, were slowly stripped away from transport, telephone services, fuel, alcohol and tobacco. The most controversial card to be played, however, was the decriminalisation of the dollar. Previously, the only Cubans allowed to use dollars were a few privileged citizens, including Party officials. If the legalisation of the dollar demonstrated that the government could not control the black market, it meant that at least it could start to syphon off some of the money circulating within it. In Havana, new dollar shops seem to open on a daily basis, each with a queue stretching down the block. Food apart, only the hard currency stores sell anything a Cuban would want to buy.

In September 1993, Decree Law 141 lifted the virtual state monopoly of production and employment by authorising limited individual private enterprise in a range of more than 100 trades from hairdressing to shoe repairs. Not all Cubans were eligible. University graduates, doctors and company directors were excluded, for fear they would abandon their prestigious but poorly-paid state jobs. A year later, the government made an equally significant concession to the changed circumstances with the introduction of markets for the sale of fresh produce and some manufactured goods at deregulated prices.

Both officially and objectively there were signs that the economy had bottomed out in 1994, but Cuba was still operating at a third of its industrial capacity and people experienced no improvement in living conditions. Levels of unemployment, estimated to be at least 25 per cent among the young, showed no signs of easing. As the following survey shows, the Cuban economy is still structurally crippled.

The Parallel Economy

A good indication of the economic well-being of any nation is provided by its currency. Officially, the Cuban *peso* is on a par with the US dollar. In 1989, its value on the parallel (or black) market was around five *pesos* to one dollar. By 1994 this had fallen to 100 *pesos*. Recent measures have helped the national currency to regain some of its value, and the government even talks about making the *peso* fully convertible. Despite such developments, the greenback is the only currency which matters.

The parallel economy has replaced the official one for almost every activity. Even committed revolutionaries are forced to deal on the black market simply to feed themselves. In 1994 it was estimated that a third of the food sent from state farms in Havana never reached market. Roadside checks by the police have increased and new laws have given the government the right to confiscate property acquired as a result of black market deals. But tackling the problem remains a hapless and politically dangerous task.

Dollars feed into this parallel economy via tourism and via the recipients of remittances from relatives in Miami. The Cuban regime has meanwhile created its own parallel dollar economy, which is essentially a legal capitalist sector. It has permitted the formation of 'private' Cuban agencies – rather like limited companies and identifiable by the initials S.A. (Sociedad Anónima)

(Julio Etchart/Reportage)

– to compete for business from foreign companies, rather than letting overseas interests dominate the legitimate hard currency market. Only trusted citizens may contribute capital to these companies, a fact which has fuelled speculation that the regime is attempting to install loyal members in the private sector in order to secure its survival if a full market economy is adopted in the future.

Agriculture

More than two-thirds of Cubans live in towns and cities, but Cuba is an essentially agricultural nation. Sugar has been the island's most significant

Fuel shortages mean that sugar production depends on antiquated technology   (Emily Hatchwell)

crop since the Conquest, and still covers more than 50 per cent of cultivated land. The oil-for-sugar swap with the USSR, while beneficial, also locked the island into the monoculture it had hoped to escape. Today, Cuba is less diversified economically than it was in 1958. With no guaranteed market and fluctuating prices, Cuba's dependence on sugar is a millstone around its neck. Furthermore, recent harvests like those in 1993 and 1994 (which both yielded 4 million tons against an average of nearer 7 million tons), have been poor due partly to bad weather but mainly to shortages of petrol and spare parts for machinery. Sugar exports, which in 1992 accounted for 65 per cent of hard currency earnings, have since dropped to just 40 per cent.

Because of fuel and spare parts shortages, an increasing proportion of sugar-cane must be cut by machete rather than by machine, a labour-intensive task which requires the large-scale mobilisation (not always voluntary) of extra workers from the cities. The improvement in services in the towns since the Revolution has resulted in a dramatic population shift from the countryside, a phenomenon common to many Latin American nations in recent decades. The government has tried to correct the situation in view of falling agricultural production. Thousands of youngmen now do obligatory agricultural rather than military service, with perks offered to encourage them to stay on afterwards and marry local women. The so-called Plan Turquino has been set up to repopulate Cuba's mountainous areas, in particular to aid the production of coffee in the Sierra Maestra. Much to the chagrin of most Cubans, for whom it is a passion, coffee is one of the country's largest agricultural exports, leaving little for local ration books. Nor do they see much of the island's most celebrated product, tobacco. Cubans are a nation of smokers but the best quality tobacco leaves, which grow around Pinar del Río in western Cuba, are reserved for the Cohibas and other brands of cigar which are strictly for export.

In terms of production for the population, as opposed to export, the figures make depressing reading. In 1992, the last year for which data are available, the country produced 69 per cent less pork, 89 per cent less powdered milk and 82 per cent fewer chickens than in 1989. Such appalling food shortages have forced the government to accept that the state sector simply cannot manage the land as effectively as private farmers and cooperatives. State farms are gradually being split up into cooperatives, and unused state land has already been made available to people for private farming. The most significant change has come with the reinstatement of farmers' markets. Allowing farmers to sell their surplus produce direct to the people at uncontrolled prices is a small but important step forward. To some extent this simply legalised the growing informal market which already existed, but the move will undoubtedly encourage the cultivation of land which has remained out of production for years due to low official prices for crops.

Bio-technology   It is hard to think of many things which are made in Cuba except rum and cigars, both firmly agriculture-based. Industrialisation has proved an elusive goal. The one area in which the country has made great strides is biotechnology. Faced with a drastic cut in the amount of medicines available after the imposition of the embargo, Castro ordered massive investment in the health sector. Almost US$150 million was spent on the construction of Havana's Centre of Genetic Engineering and Biotechnology, opened in 1986.

Progress in the field of research has been such as to enable Cuba not only to serve its own needs but also to look to the export market. Pharmaceuticals and biotechnology are at the forefront of Cuba's drive to boost its overseas trade. Cuban innovation in pharmaceuticals faces problems, however. The country's scientists have created all manner of products – from an anti-cholesterol drug called PPG to a meningitis vaccine – but export potential is limited by the fact that manufacturing standards are not up to the quality demanded by western licensing authorities. The only way ahead would appear to be associations with foreign companies.

Until now the success of such partnerships, known as 'joint ventures', has been most obvious in the field of tourism.

Tourism   Cuba is splendidly endowed to take advantage of the worldwide growth in tourism. It has all the advantages: a tropical location, beautiful beaches, a rich culture, stunning scenery and a gregarious people.

Foreign investors, to whom the Cuban government has given considerable new flexibility, have poured more money into tourism than into any other sector of the economy. In Varadero, the island's main beach resort, joint ventures between the Cuban government and overseas companies from Mexico, Germany, Spain and elsewhere have led to the construction of the country's best hotels. These large complexes can compete at the top international level. They also offer better food than can be found anywhere on the island – although the cuisine is not particularly Cuban.

But then Varadero is not typically Cuban. It is a world away from the interior of the island, where more enterprising tourists find atmospheric one-horse towns with echoes of colonial grandeur, architectural gems like Trinidad, and unrivalled tranquillity as in the Viñales valley in western Cuba. Since the big push for tourists focuses on the island's beaches, such areas still see comparatively few visitors.

Tourism has distorted the economy to the point where it is eminently worthwhile for a university professor to become a waiter. And while the industry is now overtaking sugar as a hard currency source, high net earnings are counterbalanced by dependency on hard-currency imports. Nevertheless, the statistics for the industry look impressive. After a period of such neglect that between 1960 and 1973 an average of just 3,000 tourists visited the island each year, tourism is now the only element of the economy to be growing fast (at a rate of about 10 per cent a year). The 326,000 visitors of 1989 rose to over 600,000 in 1993. The regime's prediction of two million tourists for the year 2000 may be fanciful, but it demonstrates a degree of optimism which would be hard to find in any other sector of the economy.

Although great efforts are made to insulate the tourism enclaves from the economic hardships taking place in the rest of Cuba, the problems in getting food, drink and power to resort areas cannot always be overcome. Britain's two largest tour operators have both cancelled their programmes of holidays to Cuba, citing political uncertainty as well as organisational problems. But if the island is still regarded as something of an eccentric choice by holidaymakers, this adds to, rather than detracts from, its appeal.

Improvised public transport   (M. O' Brien/Panos)

Oil and Nickel

If Fidel Castro could make one wish, it would possibly be for Cuba to discover an oil field to rival Colombia's or Venezuela's. The island already has offshore deposits, mainly along the north coast, but they are small-scale and the oil is of low quality. The high sulphur content means that the oil not only exudes a most unpleasant smell during drilling, but also corrodes the boilers and other components of the power plants. Cupet, the state oil company, has invited outside investment, but so far with limited success. Even so, domestic oil production climbs slowly.

There has been much more foreign interest in nickel, Cuba's most abundant precious mineral and its third highest-earning export after sugar and tourism. It is thought that the island has the world's fourth largest reserves of nickel, mostly in the eastern province of Holguín. After the Revolution, the managers of the largest mines left the country and took the plans with them to try and paralyse further nickel extraction. Soviet assistance helped Cuba overcome such setbacks, but production levels could be greatly improved. Joint ventures, with Canada leading the field, look set to increase production dramatically by the end of the decade.

The Economic Future

The US embargo, abetted by the collapse of communism, has reduced Cuba to an economic shambles. Yet the predicted consequence, the collapse of Castro, has not yet occurred. There even seems to be a growing sense of optimism that recovery and slow growth can be achieved.

The foreign minister, Roberto Robaina, spends much of his time flying around the world trying to encourage trade with Cuba. Pressure from Washington on potential business partners has hampered the search for new markets, but links have improved substantially with Caribbean nations and with China and Vietnam.

Because of their political backgrounds, these last two countries are perhaps the best economic models for Cuba to follow. Since they shrugged off state control, both China and Vietnam have harnessed their human potential for intense economic growth. In October 1993, Carlos Lage emphasised the primacy of the state sector and the continuing existence of the socialist framework, and emphasised that there would be no automatic copying of China and Vietnam. However, the establishment of free agricultural markets is exactly the sort of move which seems designed to emulate the success stories of Asia.

In October 1994, it was announced that all sectors, including the sugar industry, would be opened to foreign investment, demonstrating the government's admission that recovery will be impossible without investment from abroad. Accordingly, a Mexican magnate bought a half-share in the Cuban telephone system for US$1.5 billion.

As Cuba adjusts to the uncomfortable truths of poverty and privation, there are signs that the country is rejoining the capitalist world. International deals are on the increase: Colombia is to supply one-third of Cuba's oil consumption, while Mexican engineers are to restore the refinery at Cienfuegos to full capacity. With Canadian prospectors combing the country and its coasts in the search for oil, economists have begun discussing the chances of a hydrocarbon-led recovery.

The relative success of joint ventures, however, has cast the island's state-run industries in an increasingly poor light. With pragmatism in the ascendant, current government thinking is moving away from the seemingly hopeless task of improving on socialist models, and towards ways of introducing private enterprise – though without permeating the whole economy and without tainting Cuba's socialism much more. The state media has even begun educating Cubans in market culture. While the ending of the US embargo is clearly long overdue, many outside observers believe that domestic reform is just as crucial in resolving the island's economic difficulties.

5 SOCIETY

– Diversity and Equality

'No revolution could be more potent than Cuban eroticism'
Jacobo Timerman, 1987

Word spreads quickly when food arrives at the local government store. The latest consignment of eggs might be the first the neighbourhood has seen for several months. The ration book or *libreta* should guarantee Cubans a regular supply of staple goods, such as rice, beans, cooking oil and sugar, but the full monthly quota rarely materialises. Rationing in Cuba, introduced in 1962, is supposed to ensure that everyone gets an equal amount of food each month. But the meagre rations are no longer nearly enough to live on. Even the men who gather to gossip in the town squares are as likely to spend the morning discussing the latest food allowances as the latest baseball scores.

The fight for survival demonstrates the strains facing society, simultaneously pulling Cubans together and tearing them apart. People queuing for their daily bread roll exchange stories about the lengths to which some people will go in order to make money, about black marketeers passing off melted condoms for cheese on pizzas sold on the street. This shows not only the kind of creative spark which has enabled Cubans to endure the economic crisis, but also the pressures being placed on human relationships – within both the community and the family. Survival in these adverse conditions ultimately depends on trust as much as food.

Ethnic Mix Dividing Cubans – the greatest racial jumble in the Caribbean – into neat percentages of ethnicity is a hapless and also controversial activity. Official statistics suggest that the population breaks down as follows: 66 per cent white (Hispanic), 12 per cent black, 21.9 per cent mulatto (mixed Hispanic and black) and 0.1 per cent Asian. Racially-aware mulattoes and blacks dismiss such figures as indicative of a white conspiracy to diminish their importance in Cuban society. Whatever the motives, the statistics are clearly inaccurate. Some people suggest that as much as 70 per cent of the population has some black blood, although there are no statistics to substantiate this claim. Most pure blacks live in western Cuba, primarily in Havana and nearby Matanzas province.

Cubans as a whole have become decidedly darker since 1959. The economic and social changes brought by the Revolution encouraged unprecedented movement within the population, not only between the towns and country but also between the classes. Furthermore, most of the two million or so Cubans who have left the country since the 1960s are white. After Europe and Africa, China has contributed most to Cuba's racial medley. As many as 150,000 Chinese labourers arrived in the 19th century, firstly to supplement slaves and then to replace them. The government census reduces the Chinese population to around 10,000, but this suggests a misleading degree of ethnic purity. Havana's Chinatown has dwindled almost to nothing as its inhabitants have died or inter-married.

Racial Equality

Cuba would appear to be a paradise of racial harmony. Black and white kids play together happily and the kind of racial violence which afflicts Britain and the US is conspicuously absent.

In March 1959, Fidel Castro declared that he would eliminate the racial discrimination which had flourished before the Revolution. The new regime was generous with its legislation, opening up areas previously closed to blacks, such as beaches, hotels and universities, and granting them equal rights in the workplace. In 1966, Castro duly announced that race discrimination had been eradicated.

Yet losing a large percentage of Cuba's most racist citizens to the US, transforming racism into a taboo subject and removing the legal pillars of discrimination do not eliminate prejudice. Athletes and musicians are more likely to be black than white, but Hispanics dominate all other fields. Juan Almeida, vice-president of the Council of State, is a token mulatto among the sea of white faces of the Cuban leadership. Go into a hotel, and you find black employees cleaning out the rooms while paler colleagues do the higher-profile work downstairs. Black Cubans have many more educational and employment opportunities open to them than they did forty years ago, but they remain a disadvantaged group within society.

Social marginalisation, as in other countries, means that more blacks than whites resort to crime. Young black males are delinquents by definition in the eyes of the police, and ordinary Cubans will also assume that anyone who has been robbed was the victim of a black criminal.

That a Hispanic girl wanting to marry a black Cuban may still face parental pressure to dissolve the relationship stems partly from historical precedent; in colonial times, while it was perfectly acceptable for a white man to lust after a *mulata*, liaisons between white women and black men were frowned upon. It stems too from the recognition that a black husband has less hope of offering a good home than a white Cuban, as well as from more straightforward prejudice or social snobbery. Equally, black parents tend to consider marriage with a white Cuban as a 'good' match.

CUBA

The Cuban flag was first flown by anti-Spanish rebels in 1850 and was adopted when the republic became formally independent in 1902. The three blue stripes stand for the three departments into which Cuba was then divided. The white stripes symbolise the purity of independence, while the red is the blood which was shed to achieve it. The white star is a masonic emblem of independence.

Cuban flag and monument to Antonio Maceo
(Paul Schatzberger/South American Pictures)

The cathedral, old Havana
(Rolando Pujol/South American Pictures)

Havana street life
(Simon Calder)

Any Cuban can identify the names and faces of the country's extensive pantheon of national heroes, from the freedom fighters of the 19th century, such as Manuel Céspedes and Antonio Maceo, to those of the 1959 Revolution, such as Camilio Cienfuegos and Frank País. They are commemorated in the names of streets throughout the island, and in the string of anniversaries that fills the Cuban calendar. The promotion of such figures and dates helps lend legitimacy to the current regime by the sheer weight of history. Fidel Castro claims to be simply carrying on a historical process begun by the first revolutionaries to take up arms last century. He still ends most speeches with the rallying cry used during the War of Independence: 'Fatherland or Death! We will conquer!'.

One name, one face appears above all others. That of José Martí. The inspiration for the War of Independence, he has remained the standard bearer of Cubans' aspirations for change throughout the 20th century, and Fidel Castro still regularly invokes his ideas. The mass-produced bust of Martí decorates small secular shrines all over the island.

May Day celebrations in Plaza de la Revolución, Havana
(Julio Etchart/Reportage)

'Always heroic', Santiago
(M. O' Brien/Panos)

Cuba's pantheon of national heroes
(Julio Etchart/Reportage)

Che Guevara, the ultimate revolutionary icon
(Osvaldo Salas/Reportage)

The only other man honoured with a place in Havana's Plaza de la Revolución, alongside Martí, is Che Guevara. Despite abandoning most of Che's ideas, the Cuban regime continues to play on his popularity, both at home and abroad, as the world's archetypal romantic hero – though his well-known image is used more than his words.

Other great symbols of Cuba – cigars and rum cocktails – rose to worldwide fame before 1959. Even the Tropicana cabaret, the symbol of the decadence under Batista, has survived almost four decades of communism. But, like rum and tobacco, it is enjoyed more by tourists than by Cubans.

The Tropicana nighclub
(M. O' Brien/Panos)

Hemingway haunt – La Floridita, Havana
(M. O' Brien/Panos)

Granma, the national paper, *a mojito*, the national drink
(Simon Tang)

Vintage US car outside Capitol in Havana
(Julio Etchart/Reportage)

Religion   Communism has never succeeded in taking the place of religious faith in Cuba. On the other hand, the Catholic church remains weaker than anywhere else in Latin America. A mixture of persuasion and repression has reduced the number of worshippers since 1959, but the orthodox Catholic church had scant influence even before the Revolution, when it was seen by many Cubans as a hangover from colonial rule, run by Spanish priests for the benefit of the richest social classes. But the official estimate that only about one per cent of the population are practising Catholics seems extraordinarily low. The Catholic Church and the government have maintained an uneasy coexistence since their confrontation in the 1960s. A few conciliatory gestures were exchanged in the 1980s, and the admission of Catholics into the Communist Party in 1991 was seen as a major concession. The underlying bitterness remains, however, and erupted in September 1993 with the publication of a Carta Pastoral, a statement by Cuban bishops attacking the 'omnipresent official ideology' and accusing the regime of denying civil rights. To Party officials, the letter simply confirmed their view that Catholics are under the influence of counter-revolutionaries in Miami. To disaffected Cubans, it provided hope that the Catholic church might become a focus of opposition, as it had been briefly in the early days; but the church hierarchy seems reluctant to take on such a patently suicidal role.

If Cubans must turn to the heavens for comfort in difficult times – as they are doing – the regime would prefer them to turn to the Protestant church, which has made more effort than its Catholic counterpart to embrace the Revolution. The Baptists figure most prominently among the seventy or so non-Catholic churches, although the world trend for evangelism has reached Cuba too.

Santería   The religion which has most followers among all racial groups in Cuba is *santería*, a blend of African and Catholic beliefs This fusion, known as syncretism, was possible largely because colonial landowners made such poor missionaries; they were more interested in their slaves' capacity for work than their souls. Although the slaves were forbidden to practise their native religions, they managed to hide worship of their own African deities behind the names and images of Catholic saints. During the pretence of Catholic worship, the blacks subsumed aspects of Christian belief into their own religion. The term *santería* is often misused to describe all Afro-Cuban faiths, but it is simply the most widespread. According to a local saying, if you scratch a Cuban Catholic you find a *santería* believer. Two religions, one from Spain, the other from Africa, have become so mixed that no one knows where one ends and the other begins. To whom are people praying in church, a Catholic saint or an African god?

Afro-Cuban culture is most strongly represented in music   (Julio Etchart/Reportage)

Santería, also known as *Regla de Ocha*, evolved from the cult of the Yorubá or Lucumí people of Nigeria. It is not so much a faith as a way of life, in which people's lives are ruled by African deities called *orishas*. If believers have a string of bad luck, they will probably blame it on an *orisha*'s displeasure at some misdemeanor or at their neglect of religious duties. But there is no talk of sin or the final judgement.

Such an apparently irrational and unmoralising faith would seem anathema to communists, with their scientific conception of the world, but *santería* attracts even members of the Party (including, they say, Fidel Castro himself). The government has opened *santería* museums and published a string of books about it, although such official promotion is largely dictated by the need to capitalise on the interest shown in Afro-Cuban culture by tourists.

Whether thanks to the failures or the efforts of the Cuban leadership, *santería* is booming. In few other countries do you see so many young people demonstrating their religiousness by wearing the colourful *santería* necklaces and bracelets. Cynics dismiss it as a craze, charging that its adherents are attracted not so much by faith as by the music and the mystique.

Gods and Divination

Several hundred gods fill the ranks of the Yorubá pantheon, of which only about twenty feature regularly. Each is paired up with a Catholic saint according to shared attributes, although the _orisha_ or _santo_ is generally far more human (and fallible) than its Christian counterpart. For example Ochún – identified with the Catholic Virgin of Charity, the patron saint of Cuba – is the goddess of fresh water and love, but she is represented as a beautiful and flirtatious _mulata_. Dancing is one of Ochún's tools of seduction, but in _santería_ music also forms an integral part of the spiritual experience. On saints' days and other special religious occasions, people celebrate with dancing and singing and, whenever possible, alcohol.

Olofí represents the closest _santería_ equivalent to the Catholic supreme god. But the ruler of the Yorubá celestial world would be powerless without Orula, the god of wisdom, who by means of divination allows Olofí and the other _orishas_ to communicate with believers. People consult Orula before making important decisions or simply to seek advice. Strong believers may decide to leave the country or get a divorce on the basis of divination.

Santería priests or _babalawos_ (the priesthood is male-only) perform divination in their own homes. Various instruments can be used in the process, most commonly the _okpele_, a chain with eight pieces of coconut shell which when swung onto the floor can fall into any of 256 combinations. Each is a sign which carries with it numerous myths and stories amassed over centuries, and which the _babalawo_ will interpret for his client.

Sex and Marriage

Sex is Cuba's national pastime. In a country where everything is either rationed or unobtainable, sex survives as one of the few things not controlled by the state. Houses are so cramped with extended families, however, that couples with money to spare resort to spartan 'love hotels' called _posadas_ for a little privacy.

The Revolution has encouraged matrimony so successfully that in 35 years the annual number of marriages has more than doubled. Cubans are torn between the government's promotion of the family (and the material incentives available to those who tie the knot) and their own instinctively relaxed attitude towards relationships. In sharp contrast with other Latin American countries bound by Catholic morality, more than 60 per cent of Cuban babies are born out of wedlock, although this also reflects reluctance to use contraception. Abortion, which has been free and legal since 1965, is the most common method of birth control.

Cubans tend to change partners frequently, a habit reflected in the astounding fact that among Cubans aged 25-40, 60 per cent of marriages end in divorce. The government has made getting a divorce cheap and easy, and the trauma of the experience rarely seems to put Cubans off trying marriage again.

Women

The communist regime has markedly improved women's access to jobs. Having made up less than a fifth of the workforce before the Revolution, women now represent almost 40 per cent. Women have also broken into traditionally male-dominated spheres such as medicine, although they have had less success at entering the upper echelons in any sphere; just three of the 25 members of the Party's Politburo are women.

The Federación de Mujeres de Cuba (FMC), the Cuban Women's Federation, was set up to mobilise women politically rather than crack the *machismo* inherent in Cuban society. However, it has played a role in formulating some remarkably progressive legislation – in particular, the Family Code passed in 1974, which set out the responsibilities of married couples and gave men and women both equal rights and responsibilities for child-rearing, education and even housework. Such a law cannot be enforced easily, however, and attitudes change slowly. Most Cuban families still celebrate a daughter's 15th birthday in special style to announce her coming of age and, traditionally, her readiness for marriage. In or out of wedlock, so many women have children before they are twenty, that they lose out on the career oppportunities that the Revolution opened up for them.

While it is still the case that most men believe it is acceptable for husbands, but not for wives, to be unfaithful, the rise in the divorce rate springs partly from the fact that women now feel more confident about putting an end to unhappy relationships.

Homo-sexuality

Fidel Castro once said that a homosexual could never embody the characteristics of a true revolutionary. You cannot be glad to be gay in Cuba, though life has improved since the days when hundreds of homosexuals were marched off to labour camps to rid them of their supposed moral laxity.

The government's greater tolerance towards homosexuality is often held up as evidence of a more widespread ideological openness. Published in 1989, *El bosque, el lobo, el hombre nuevo* ('The Wood, the Wolf, the New Man'), a story written by Senel Paz about a sophisticated gay man and his friendship with a young communist, was the first book in years to deal with homosexuality. The 1993 screen version, *Fresa y chocolate* ('Strawberry and Chocolate'), caused even more of a stir. But neither the book nor the film did much to reduce homophobia in a society where conventional and heterosexual characteristics have been reinforced by communist morality. *Maricón*, the local word for gay, is often used to describe a spineless (heterosexual) man, though thankfully gay-bashing is not a common Cuban pursuit. The state provides no publicly gay bars or clubs, and gay men and lesbians who are open about their sexuality find certain professions closed to them; homosexual teachers, for example, are thought to distort the image of what a good socialist should be. Still, the biggest day-to-day problem for most gay Cubans is the lack of understanding in the family home.

Education   José Martí wrote that to be educated is the only way to be free. In Cuba the duty of teachers is to turn out well-educated socialists. The education-or-indoctrination debate aside, Castro's regime has replaced a system which provided a decent education only for the rich with one which offers free schooling for everyone and has achieved literacy levels that are the envy of developing countries around the world.

At the United Nations in 1960, Castro declared that he proposed to eliminate illiteracy in Cuba. Not long afterwards, he despatched more than 250,000 teachers and school children into the Cuban interior to teach the peasants to read and write. In a staggering feat of voluntary fervour, illiteracy was reduced from 23.6 per cent to 3.9 per cent by the end of 1962, providing a benchmark for the regime's achievements.

The slogan 'Every worker a student, every student a worker' encapsulates the other main thrust in Castro's educational vision. This ideal prompted the introduction in 1971 of one of the world's most daring experiments in education: the 'School in the Country', where students split their time between classes and agricultural work. The Cuban leader's obsession with science has also meant that arts degree courses have been sharply reduced, but the number of universities has rocketed, from three in 1959 to an impressive forty today.

The austerity package known as the Special Period has pushed education into crisis. Illiteracy levels have risen and truancy is on the increase as the state struggles to provide books and public transport. In Havana, primary school children in their maroon uniforms hang around outside hotels begging tourists for dollars and pens.

Healthcare   The achievements of the Revolution in the field of healthcare have reached almost legendary status. Cuba has created not only a medical service accessible to the entire population, free of charge, but possibly the most extensive health system in Latin America.

Before 1959 healthcare was advanced, but few had access to it: 60 per cent of Cuba's 6,000 doctors worked in the capital, and half of them left after the Revolution. From such inauspicious beginnings, Cuba now has a vast army of doctors and a network of polyclinics which extends into every corner of the island. The country's infant mortality rates – which fell from 60 deaths per 1,000 in 1958 to 12 in 1990 – put Cuba in a league with developed

Domino players, Old Havana   (M. O' Brien/Panos)

countries and above parts of the US. Average life expectancy in Cuba is 75 years, compared with a Third World average closer to 57.

The main causes of death in Cuba (cancer, strokes and heart disease) are equally uncharacteristic of a developing nation. Vaccination drives over the last thirty years have eradicated malaria, polio and tetanus, and have greatly reduced the incidence of other diseases from tuberculosis to meningitis. Advanced medical science has developed to the point where organ transplants and laser treatment are commonplace and, in theory, available free to any citizen. People also travel to Cuba from abroad for specialist medical care. Several hundred Chernobyl children are still on the island undergoing treatment against radiation unavailable to them at home.

But healthcare, the jewel in Cuba's revolutionary crown, has been crumbling since 1989. The flagship Hermanos Almeijeiras Hospital in Havana is kept in reasonable shape, but elsewhere stories of dirty syringes and sticky tape used in the absence of suture material reverberate around the wards. In May 1994 a team of Spanish health experts returned from Cuba saying that life expectancy was shortening by the year. Medical aid from abroad has been vital in helping to shore up the health system, although some of this gets sucked into the dollar whirlpool of the central economy. Most medicines on the market are sold in hard currency shops, out of reach of the majority of Cubans. Local people must rely instead on local pharmacies which look more like museums than dispensing chemists.

Aids

In line with its remarkable record in other spheres of medicine, the number of people infected with HIV and Aids in Cuba is very low. According to official statistics in 1993, 147 Cubans had died of Aids and there were 987 carriers of the HIV virus, of whom 702 were men and 285 women.

Cuba's methods to prevent the spread of Aids (Sida in Spanish) have caused considerable controversy. This has arisen because of the government's introduction of compulsory Aids tests for adults and the use of sanatoria, where anyone infected with the virus is isolated from the community. Protestors, mostly from abroad, claim that such a policy is a violation of human rights. The Cuban government believes instead that by isolating patients it is defending the rights of the millions of Cubans who are not infected. Castro has in fact recently encouraged a less restrictive regime in the sanatoria. Aids patients considered fit and sexually responsible are allowed to go out to work and spend more time at home.

In Cuba, as elsewhere, Aids was first dismissed as a gay disease, but half the infections are among heterosexuals. In 98 per cent of cases, the virus is transmitted through sex. Education campaigns have concentrated on promoting the use of condoms, but still only about six per cent of Cubans use what is known locally as *el quitasensaciones*, 'the killjoy'. Aids remains just a remote danger to the average Cuban.

Living with Tourism

The government which abolished Christmas now decks out its hotels in tinsel and fairy lights and holds special parties for the tourists on 25 December. Having condemned tourism as the epitome of pre-1959 decadence, the government has embraced the industry like a long-lost lover. Fidel Castro defends such a turnaround with statements about economic necessity, but he cannot justify so easily the exclusion of Cubans from many services offered to foreigners. The official line is that if local people were allowed to stay in tourist hotels, there would be less room for foreigners and therefore less hard currency to buy food for the Cuban people. The sacrifice must be borne for the sake of socialism.

There is the uncomfortable sense that life has gone full circle. As in the Batista days, hotels are bastions of the socially privileged. Most tourist hotels, particularly in Havana, admit Cubans only if they are invited by a foreigner. To many Cubans this system of so-called 'tourist apartheid' is simply evidence that they are treated like second-class citizens in their own country. A tourist who is robbed receives more attention from the police than a Cuban; the dollar restaurants serve food that the average Cuban has not tasted in months; and a typical night out for most locals is a stroll around the streets, while tourists can dance and drink into the early hours. Tourism, which Castro hopes will save Cuba economically, is socially divisive.

Cubans of all descriptions seek out tourists, some for friendship, others for a free drink or maybe in the hope of marriage and an easy escape. As the economic situation has worsened, more and more women have turned to prostitution. The so-called *jineteras*, dismissed by the press as 'morally sick' amateurs doing it for clothes rather than real necessities, are one sector of society which enters hotels without problem. This has laid the regime open to accusations that it is tolerating sex tourism, already a boom industry in Havana and the resort of Varadero.

Crime

Street children do not exist, drug-addiction is only a small problem, and the visitor will not find the sprawling shanties that afflict cities elsewhere in Latin America and the Caribbean. Violent crimes such as rape are rare.

But Cuba's relatively crime-free society has been undermined by economic crisis, tourism and frustration. The majority of Cubans break the law every day simply to survive, by buying food on the black market. Beggars, a rarity just five years ago, are now commonplace in Havana. The opening of new shops catering for Cubans and tourists with dollars makes people increasingly consumer-conscious and unsympathetic towards the government's calls for sacrifice. The number of bag-snatchings from foreigners is rising and the police presence in tourist centres has been stepped up considerably. The police can do little about bicycle theft, however, which is the most common crime against impoverished Cubans. People who cycle at night risk being ambushed, so now some ride with a machete strapped to their crossbar.

Visitors to the island should bear in mind that the rise in crime began from an extraordinarily low base. Many Westerners find that Cuba is by far the safest country they have ever visited. More Cubans commit crimes against the government than against tourists or each other.

6   CULTURE

– Caribbean Fusion

'Here everything is resolved with drums and beer'
La Bella de la Alhambra

Few Cubans would hesitate to swap a local *guayabera* shirt for a baseball cap, or a pack of local Popular cigarettes for a packet of Marlboro (and not just for the taste). Leaving aside politics, Cubans love North American culture. They love their own, too, with its unmistakable style forged from African and Spanish roots. The regime has been accused of trying to downgrade Afro-Cuban culture into mere folklore and of continuing the old distinction between 'high' white culture (such as drama and ballet) and 'low' black culture (popular music and dance). There is no doubt where the preference of most Cubans lies, although ballet draws big crowds. This is thanks mainly to the work of Alicia Alonso, now in her seventies, who founded the National Ballet and enjoys the affectionate title 'First Lady of Cuba'.

As early as 1961, Fidel Castro told writers and artists: 'Everything within the Revolution, nothing against the Revolution.' Intellectuals were there to serve socialism and the masses, not the élite. Cuba lost fine people as some of the best and boldest writers, artists and musicians chose exile rather than artistic asphyxiation, oblivion or forced labour. Cuba sank into cultural isolation, cut off from all but Eastern European influences. Interestingly, despite 30 years' involvement in the island, the USSR had no lasting impact on Cuban culture.

Cuban intellectuals have learned to work within the parameters set by the government, a process of self-censorship almost as efficient as the official kind. Others have chosen to collaborate, in realisation that this was the only possible route to a career in the arts. The long-running debate between hardliners and those in favour of greater artistic freedom has brought some relaxation in the government line, but creative success is still often due more to political than artistic merit.

The most beneficial effect of the Revolution on culture has been the broadening of cultural life to reach the entire Cuban population. Every sizeable town now has its own museum, cultural centre, theatre and cinema, to which access is either free or very cheap. Unfortunately, many of these have been casualties of the Special Period and a cultural evening for most Cubans is a night in front of the television, where educational programmes are interlaced with music videos, pirated movies from North America and Brazilian soaps – during which the country falls into rapt silence.

Salsa rhythms in Havana
(Rolando Pujol/South
American Pictures)

Music

Cuba has one of the world's richest and most original musical traditions. It is not just a passion, but an intrinsic part of the Cuban temperament. The country's music has been a notable influence abroad over the last fifty years, although international isolation, imposed by the Revolution and the embargo together, has done Cuban musicians no favours. The best groups, such as Irakere, Cuba's top jazz band, now do most of their recording abroad and can therefore reach a wider audience, but back home the opportunities are minimal. In Cuba, few resources are available, and the state evaluating committees keep tight control over the kind of music played.

From *Son* to *Salsa*

Fernando Ortíz, the first person to undertake serious research into Afro-Cuban culture, wrote that most of the island's music sprang from 'the love affair of African drums and Spanish guitar.' Indeed, it was only with the absorption of blacks into society following the abolition of slavery that music really took off in the island. The white middle classes were almost schizophrenic in their music appreciation in the early 20th century, fascinated by the intoxicating rhythms produced by the blacks, yet resistant to abandoning their more sedate dances.

Son, which hit Havana in around 1910, was one of the earliest manifestations of the fusion of Hispanic and African music, and it has inspired Cuban musicians ever since. It developed among guitar-strumming troubadours in Oriente, but rapidly permeated the mainstream music scene. A double bass, trumpets, bongoes and other percussion instruments joined the traditional accompaniment of a three-stringed guitar called a *tres*. The Septeto Nacional of Ignacio Piñeiro was one of the first orchestras to make *son* famous in the 1920s. Two decades later Benny Moré, nicknamed 'The Barbarian of Rhythm', became a legend in his own time as Cuba's best-loved *son* artist.

The original *son* is of enduring popularity, but it has also spawned numerous variations from mambo, which swept the world in the 1950s, to the more recent salsa. The latter emerged in New York in the 1960s, but few would dispute its origins in Cuban *son*. Salsa has had its ups and downs – in the 1980s a romantic variant known as salsa erótica was slammed as a betrayal of the essentially *macho* character of the genre. But in Cuba, bands such as NG La Banda, Sierra Maestra, Issac Delgado and Los Van Van have rejuvenated salsa, bringing in new influences while never losing sight of its essential ingredients: the brass section, syncopated percussion and catchy choruses. NG La Banda's streetwise lyrics and eminently danceable rhythms have earned it a cult following at home.

Afro-Cuban Music   Most music on the island could be described as Afro-Cuban – African rhythms and songs have become the basis for much of the country's jazz and popular music – but the term is normally used to describe only the purest forms of black music. These sound more like the authentic rhythms of Africa than those of a Latin American disco.

Rumba, the most accessible Afro-Cuban music, has been around since the end of the 19th century. It first emerged among urban blacks, mostly in Havana and nearby Matanzas, where it absorbed influences from African religious music. One of the most famous *rumba* dances, the *columbia*, is a fast and almost acrobatic solo man's dance based on the moves of the devils which feature in certain ceremonies of the Afro-Cuban cult of Abakuá.

African rhythms remain in their most unadulterated form in Yorubá ritual music. Complex and intoxicating rhythms designed to invoke the gods are played out on hourglass-shaped drums called *batás*, which are themselves revered as religious objects. They are accompanied by a soloist and chorus singing songs of praise (known as *cantos*) and dancing. While some practitioners dismiss the state's Conjunto Nacional Folklórico (the National Folklore Group) as a gimmick, it has undoutedly helped to popularise Yorubá music.

The July carnival in Santiago de Cuba, one of the best cultural events in Latin America, used to be the most vibrant expression of Afro-Cuban music in the country. Sadly, the nation's carnival celebrations have not escaped the effects of the economic crisis, and in 1990 were postponed until further notice.

Youth Music

You won't often find *roqueros* or *freakies* dancing salsa. Rockers and hippies (respectively) prefer to grow their hair long, wear tatty jeans and sway to American rock. Some Cubans have undoubtedly turned to foreign music as a reaction to the state's involvement even in the sacrosanct sphere of music, but listening to the Beatles or Santana is no longer the gesture of protest that it was in the early days. The reality is that a home-grown rock movement simply hasn't emerged to satisfy Cuba's youth.

After the Revolution, politically-minded musicians breathed life into an old ballad tradition and created Nueva Trova, the only musical movement to have emerged since 1959. Silvio Rodríguez and Pablo Milanés, its main exponents, did not go down well with the regime initially, and Rodríguez even spent time in a labour camp. Both have since made their peace with Fidel Castro and are regularly in demand to entertain the crowds on important political anniversaries.

In the 1980s, the role of protest singer was taken up by Carlos Varela. With his beard and black hat, he veers more towards folk than rock, but he voices the frustrations of some young Cubans, above all their desire for change. Varela's music was banned for a time, but since he has never called for violent protest some radio stations now give him airtime, and he has shared a stage with Castro himself.

Cinema

The Cuban regime has used cinema, like the rest of the media, as an instrument of political education, but Cuban films have a justifiably high reputation on the world's screens. A series of talented directors, such as Humberto Solás and Tomás Gutiérrez Alea, are among the most creative artists to have worked successfully under the Revolution. Enrique Pineda Barnet's *La Bella de la Alhambra* ('The Beauty of the Alhambra'), which recounts the fortunes of an unsuccessful chorus girl in Havana during the 1920s, received an Oscar nomination in 1991.

Cubans adore the movies. They will queue for hours to see a new release and applaud enthusiastically during a good film. Despite the shadow cast by the Instituto Cubano del Arte y la Industria Cinematográficos (ICAIC),

Havana Style

Old *Habaneros* remember their city as the grandest and most beautiful in Latin America. Looking down on central Havana's rooftops now, you would be forgiven for thinking you had landed in war-ravaged Sarajevo. The city is not just peeling at the

Restored street in Old Havana

(Rolando Pujol/South American Pictures)

edges, but crumbling and falling apart. The preservation of old architecture never featured on the list of Marxist priorities. Indeed, following the Revolution, the policy was consciously to neglect the capital given that it had received earlier governments' undivided attention for years, to the detriment of the rest of the country.

In 1982 most of central Havana was added to UNESCO's list of World Heritage Sites. Restorers are now working feverishly to make up for lost time. They have already restored the cream of the capital's early buildings, which rub shoulders with overcrowded and decrepit homes along the narrow streets of Old Havana. The unmistakable look of the city's colonial buildings, with their solid, tropical grace, derives from the fusion of the *mudéjar* style – the blend of Christian and Muslim traditions brought by craftsman from Andalucía in Spain – with more sophisticated baroque influences. The 18th-century house of Conde de Casa Bayona, in Cathedral Square, is a typical *Habanero* colonial home. The central courtyard is enclosed by an arcaded gallery with walls painted golden yellow and wooden balustrades icy blue: a sea-and-sand colour combination which recurs all over Old Havana. Upstairs, the *mudéjar* carpenters made some of the city's finest ceilings, the so-called *alfarjes*. Geometric star patterns decorate the beams – an Islamic representation of the universe which the Christian residents did not seem to mind.

the Cuban Institute of Film Art and Industry, directors have managed to retain some autonomy and tackle important social issues head on. But the timing has to be correct. The film *Alicia en el pueblo de maravillas* ('Alice in Wonderland'), made during the upheavals in Eastern Europe, was taken off the screens after just four days, during which police harassed members of the audience who cheered at the jibes against the system. Several years on, Tomás Gutiérrez Alea's *Fresa y chocolate* was promoted more than any other film in recent history, its overtly critical approach being described in the official Cuban press as 'constructive criticism'.

An award for *Fresa y chocolate* at the Berlin Film Festival in 1994 was received gladly. Cinema is important for Cuba's prestige abroad, culturally and politically, as well as a source of hard currency. It is significant that Cuba has not sacrificed the annual Latin American Film Festival to the Special Period. It draws a large international audience and provides a springboard for the release of Cuban films made in increasingly difficult conditions.

Literature   The Argentinian journalist, Jacobo Timerman, wrote that 'If it is true that every Cuban knows how to read and write, it is likewise true that every Cuban has nothing to read and must be very cautious about what he writes.' In most Cuban bookshops, the complete works of Lenin gather dust on half-empty shelves alongside dreary tomes about crop management and Marxist economics.

Writers in Cuba have largely missed out on the flowering of Latin American fiction. The dazzling literary life that characterised Havana during the 'pseudo-republic' died in 1959. Alejo Carpentier and Nicolás Guillén, the island's two greatest authors, lived well into the Revolution but they wrote most of their best works before the rebels' triumph. Alejo Carpentier (1904-1980) was distinctly avant-garde in his imagery, and a good many readers find his surrealist novels virtually incomprehensible. The poetry of Nicolás Guillén (1902-89) is much more accessible. A mulatto by descent and conviction, he used musical rhythms to cut his poetry to a distinct Afro-Cuban mould. Guillén, Cuba's National Poet and a lifelong communist, wrote many poems in praise of the Revolution's achievements and was a loyal participant in the country's cultural and political life.

The first generation of writers to mature under communism continued to draw inspiration from Afro-Cuban culture. Cuba's most important living author, Miguel Barnet, is one of the island's few modern writers to have an international reputation. His best-known book, *Biografía de un cimarrón*, published in 1967 and later translated as 'The Autobiography of a Runaway Slave', began a small trend for the so-called 'testimonial novel', which recounts the life of a living person in the individual's own words. More recently, younger authors such as Senel Paz and Reinaldo González have grappled with new and grittier issues ranging from Aids to tourism.

Cubans are told that sport is an antidote to vice, but for most of them it's more like sex or music: a national passion and, in difficult times, an escape.

Baseball is Cuba's number one sport   (Julio Etchart/Reportage)

Sport

The regime has incorporated sport into its moral code with mixed success (the Cubans bet on everything), but it has also raised the country's sporting achievement to unimaginable heights. Before the Revolution, Cubans were known for their success on the baseball pitch and in the boxing ring, but had only ever won six Olympic gold medals. In 1976, at the Montréal games, Cuba came eighth in the medal table with six golds; it has done even better since. In terms of population, these results were great achievements.

Sport is a matter of national pride, and despite Cuba's crippled economy, Castro refused to renege on his promise to host the Pan-American Games in 1991. The Villa Pan Americana, built just outside Havana for the tournament, stands as a monument to the leadership's determination to defend the island's international image. The games proved to be a great success since Cuba walked off with 140 gold medals, the first time a Latin American country had ever defeated the US.

Success in sports brings lasting prestige as well as material benefits. The heavyweight boxer Teófilo Stevenson, three-time world champion and Olympic gold-medallist, retired from competition in 1988 but remains a national hero. Javier Sotomayor, currently the world champion in the high-jump, was elected a deputy in the last National Assembly. Given that sportspeople form a recognised élite, it was a severe blow to the regime when 40 members of the Cuban team at the Central American and Caribbean Games in Puerto Rico in 1993 decided to defect.

Baseball   For some Cubans, sport means a game of dominoes. But for most it means *pelota*, or baseball. Kids play it in the street from the moment they can walk. Adults argue about it every day under the trees in Havana's central square. Men and women together scream and shout from the terraces during matches, and the country grinds to a halt during the climax of the National Series. This usually involves two of the big four teams: Industriales (of Havana), Santiago, Pinar del Río and Villa Clara.

The Americans brought baseball to Cuba in the 1860s. It caught on so quickly that by 1872 Havana had founded its own baseball club. The Spanish banned it at first, on the pretext that the Cubans used games as a cover for conspiring against them, so the sport failed to develop seriously until after independence. From the 1940s, the Cuban baseball team was often champion of the World Amateur Series, and the country's top players infiltrated major-league baseball in the US. Indeed, the New York Giants once tried to recruit Fidel Castro himself. Cuban players have lost none of their panache and generally compete well at the international level. In the 1992 Olympics, the Cuban team breezed through the baseball competition; many of its top players are being eyed enviously by US teams, anxious to attract them to the professional game.

CONCLUSION

In the Spanish-run *Habana Libre* Hotel, foreign tourists enjoy a coke and a ham sandwich, paid for in dollars and costing the equivalent of twice the average monthly salary in Cuba. Across the street, local people queue for two or three hours at the state-run Coppelia ice cream parlour, where they pay for a cone in local *pesos*. Is this what the Cuban Revolution was fought for?

In 1959, amidst the euphoria which followed the arrival of the idealistic young revolutionaries to power, people called their offspring Libertad (Freedom) and Fidel in honour of the Revolution. Some Cubans still worship their leader as a revolutionary hero; but others dismiss him as an an anachronistic despot. Yet while Cubans cannot agree over the nature of their president, few can imagine what life could be like without him.

Abroad, Cuba is defined largely in terms of its leader – and nowhere more so than in the US. Bill Clinton, the ninth US president to square up to Fidel Castro, must dream of being the one who sees the demise of Cuban communism and its leader. If the fate of both is inextricably linked, then Castro will be concerned that communism in Cuba may have already entered its final act.

As the pace towards market reform quickens, Cubans are looking anxiously towards the lesson of Russia and the rest of the former Soviet bloc. The changes ~~changes~~ there resulted in a huge fall in living standards; if the same thing happened in Cuba, the results would be cataclysmic. But those optimists who remain in Cuba believes slow growth can be achieved.

Ironically, it will be easier for Cuba to carry out a process of manageable change with the embargo in place. With US interests prevented from exerting pressure, Cuba may be able to proceed at its own speed. Only the embargo separates the island from McDonalds and Dunkin' Donuts, but when US businesses return to Cuba, they will meet stiff competition from European and other foreign companies which have already developed business interests.

The regime in Havana is insistent on the continuing existence of a socialist framework. Everyone, from the hardliners to the quasi-liberals, wishes to protect Cuba's welfare achievements since 1959. But while the long-term objectives may be the same, they argue about the means to achieve them. The debate is gathering in urgency, but the regime is encouraged by the liberalisation so far. 'People realise there is a way out', says Ricardo Alarcón. Roberto Robaina, another man who is likely to play an important role in the future, has said 'We don't need another Fidel.' But his is a hard act to follow. All that is certain is that a future without Castro, eagerly awaited or dreaded, will take Cuba into as yet uncharted waters.

FURTHER READING AND ADDRESSES

Arenas, R., *Before Night Falls: A Memoir*. New York, 1993.
Baloyra, E.A. & J.A. Morris, *Conflict and Change in Cuba*. New Mexico, 1993.
Barnet, M., *The Autobiography of a Runaway Slave, Esteban Montejo*. London,
Bethell, Leslie, *Cuba, A Short History*. Cambridge, 1993.
Brandon, G., *Santería from Africa to the New World*. Indiana, 1993.
Cabrera Infante, G., *Mea Cuba*. London, 1994.
Calder S. & E. Hatchwell, *Travellers Survival Kit: Cuba*. Oxford, 1993.
Cardoso, E. & A. Helwege, *Cuba After Communism*. Massachussets, 1992.
Castro, F., *Che: A Memoir*. Melbourne, 1994.
Gunn, G., *Cuba in Transition: Options for US Policy*. New York, 1993.
Halperin, M., *Return to Havana: The Decline of Cuban Society under Castro*. Nashville, 1994.
Helly, D., *The Cuban Commission Report - A Hidden History of the Chinese in Cuba (1876)*. Baltimore, 1993.
Liss, S.B., *Fidel! Castro's Political and Social Thought*. Colorado, 1994. Oppenheimer, A., *Castro's Final Hour*. New York, 1992.
Orozco, R., *Cuba Roja: Cómo viven los cubanos con Fidel Castro*. Madrid, 1993.
Pérez, L.A. Jr, *Cuba: Between Reform and Revolution*. New York, 1988.
Pérez Sarduy, P. & J. Stubbs, *Afrocuba*. London, 1993.
Pérez Stable, M., *The Cuban Revolution - Origins, Course and Legacy*. New York, 1993.
Quirk, R.E., *Fidel Castro*. New York, 1993.
Rieff, D., *The Exile: Cuba in the Heart of Miami*. London, 1994.
Szulc, T., *Fidel, A Critical Portrait*. London, 1989.
Timerman, J., *Cuba: A Journey*. London, 1994.
Williams, S., *Cuba, the Land, the Culture, the History, the People*. London, 1994.

FICTION

Cabrera Infante, G., *View of Dawn in the Tropics*. London, 1990.
Carpentier, A., *Explosion in a Cathedral*. London, 1971.

García, Cristina, *Dreaming in Cuban*. New York, 1992.
Greene, G., *Our Man in Havana*. London, 1994.
Hemingway, E., *The Old Man and the Sea*. London, 1994.

ADDRESSES

Cuban Embassy
167 High Holborn
London WC1V 6PA
Tel 071-240 2488.
(tourist office at same address, Tel 0171-379-1706)

Cuba Solidarity Campaign
c/o Red Rose Club
129 Seven Sisters Road
London N7 7QG
Tel 0171-263-6452

Center for Cuban Studies
124 W. 23 Street,
New York, NY 10011
Tel (212) 242-0559

Global Exchange, Cuba Project
2017 Mission Street, Ste. 303,
San Francisco, CA 94110
Tel (415) 255-7296

Regent Holidays
15 John Street,
Bristol BS1 2HR
Tel 0117-9211711
(tour operator specialising in Cuba)

Progressive Tours
12 Porchester Place
London W2 2BS
Tel 0171-262-1676
(specialist tour operator)

Journey Latin America
14-16 Devonshire Road,
Chiswick, London W4 2HD
Tel 0181-747-3108
(Tours and flights)

FACTS AND FIGURES

A GEOGRAPHY

Official name: República de
Cuba.
Situation: Cuba lies in the
Caribbean Sea, between 19 49'-23
18' N and 74 8' and 84 57' W; it is
the largest of the Greater Antilles,
extending 1,250km in length,
191km at its widest point, 31km at
its narrowest.
Surface area: 114,524km2 (UK
245,000km2).
Administrative division: 14
provincias, divided into 169
municipios.
Capital: Ciudad de la Habana
(Havana), population 2,100,000
(1989 estimate).
*Other large towns (population
1989 estimate x 1,000):* Santiago
de Cuba (405), Camaguey (283),
Holguín (228), Guantánamo (200),
Santa Clara (194) and Cienfuegos
(123).
Infrastructure (1987 figures):
13,112km paved roads, 33,443km
unpaved. Paved roads are poorly
maintained but a small volume of
traffic means wear and tear are
minimal. The most important
roads are the Ocho Vías, an eight-
lane motorway which runs west
from Havana to Pinar del Río and
eastward to Camaguey
(incomplete), and the older
Carretera Central (1,144km), which
crosses the entire country from
Pinar del Río to Santiago and runs
through the middle of many
towns and cities; the Vía Blanca

Time difference:

London 12.00 noon
Havana 7.00 a.m.
Washington DC 7.00 a.m.

connects Havana and Varadero.
Cuba has 14,519km of railtrack;
9,648 of this is used by the sugar
industry, the rest being run for
public service by *Ferrocarriles
de Cuba*. The main international
airports are Havana, Varadero,
Santiago, Camaguey and
Holguín; the state airline, *Cubana
de Aviación*, operates
international and domestic flights.
The main ports are Havana,
Santiago, Cienfuegos and
Matanzas.

Relief and landscape: wide and
fertile plains predominate in Cuba
(60% of which is under 200m
above sea level); about a third of
the island is mountainous; the
principal range is the Sierra
Maestra, which extends 240km in
the south-eastern corner of the
island; its tallest peak is Pico
Turquino (1,982m); the highest
point in the Escambray mountains
north of Trinidad is Pico San Juan
(1,056m); the Cordillera de
Guaniguanico in Pinar del Río

province includes the Sierra de los Organos, with its famous mogotes, large limestone humps which rise dramatically out of the flat tobacco fields of the Viñales valley and conceal caves and subterranean rivers; Cuba has more than 200 rivers, but most are short and shallow, average length 40km; the longest is Río Cauto, which extends for 370km along the northern edge of the Sierra Maestra, although the best waterfalls are along Río Hanabanilla in central Cuba; the south coast is scattered with marshes, the largest being the protected Ciénaga de Zapata in Matanzas province, and dense mangrove forest can be found in places; by contrast, the northern coast is mostly rocky, except for the central part which has some of the island's finest white sand beaches, most famously at Varadero near Havana and Santa Lucía near Holguín; Cuba is surrounded by more than 1,600 tiny islands and keys; Isla de la Juventud is the largest (2,330km2); coral reefs skirt the main island, the longest stretching for some 400km along the north coast of Camagu ey province; the water is very clear and perfect for diving.
Temperature and rainfall: Cuba has a tropical climate, with a rainy season from May to October and a

dry season from November to April; the temperatures are cooler during the dry season, but there is always plenty of sun; temperatures across the island vary very little, ranging from around 16C in January to near 32C in August, but as a rule hover closer to the annual average of 25C; increased humidity in the summer brings the main difference. North-easterly trade winds temper the heat in all but the extreme summer months of July and August, which are sultry and particularly unpleasant in Havana. The average annual rainfall is 1,515mm. Torrential rainstorms are possible at any time, but mostly in summer and autumn. Oriente tends to receive less rain than the west.
Earthquakes and hurricanes: from September to November, Cuba is vulnerable to very strong hurricanes, when winds can reach 300km/hour and bring torrential rain; like many Caribbean islands, Cuba has suffered devastation by hurricanes; more than 4,000 people died in Hurricane Flora in 1963; better advance warning means that subsequent storms have brought lower death tolls but warnings cannot prevent crop devastation; the so-called Storm of the Century in 1993 killed about 200 people and flattened crops, doing millions of dollars worth of damage; earthquakes have affected mainly

Trinidad and Santiago in the past, but they are very rare.
Flora and fauna: Cuba has about 8,000 species of plant but does not have lush vegetation to compete with Central and South America, although there are small isolated pockets of tropical rainforest in the Sierra Maestra and Escambray mountains; about a quarter of the island's surface is wooded, but only a fraction of the species (including cedar and mahogany) used abundantly by colonial furniture-makers survive; on the other hand, Cuba has an estimated 70 million palm trees, among the highest such concentrations in the world; the elegant royal palm, with its smooth, silvery trunk, is seen everywhere from sugar plantations to courtyards in the centre of Havana; Cuba has about 300 species of birds (7% endemic), including parrots, the Cuban Trogon, which has red, white and blue plumage - the colours of the Cuban flag - and is the national bird, and the bee hummingbird, the smallest in the world; Cuba has no poisonous snakes and few large mammals living in the wild, though wild boar and deer are found in the Guanahacabibes peninsula in Pinar del Río province, and monkeys live in some isolated areas; the protected Zapata swamps are home to thousands of crocodiles.

B   POPULATION

Population (1993): 10,900,000 (1970: 8.5 million).
Annual population growth: 1970-1980: 1.3%; 1980-1990: 0.9%; 1990-1995 0.9%; projected population in 2000 is 11.5 million.
Population density (1992): 97 inhabitants per km2.

Urbanisation (1992): 75% (1970: 60.2%).
Fertility: a Cuban woman has an average of 1.9 children (1992).
Age structure: one in three Cubans is under 26.
Birthrate (1992): 17 per 1,000.
Mortality rate (1992): 7 per 1,000.

Infant mortality (1993): 9.4 per 1,000 live births (1960: 65 per 1,000).
Average life expectancy (1992): men 73.5 years; women 77.4 years.
Average household (1981 census): 4 persons.
Doctors (1992): 1 doctor per 231 inhabitants.

Daily per capita calorie consumption (1993): 1,780 (compared with 2,845 in 1989 and the UN recommended level of 3,000).
Literacy (1992): 96% (men); 94% women.
Education (1989): 95% enrolled at primary school; 89% at secondary school; 17.2% at tertiary level.
Universities (1989): there are 40 universities; enrolment 2,304 students per 100,000 inhabitants.
Social Development Index, UNDP Human Development Index (1994): 89th position (in 'medium human development' category); UK 10th, US 8th positions; total 173 positions.
Ethnic composition: officially 66% Hispanic, 12% black, 21.9% mulatto (mixed Hispanic and black) and 0.1% Asian.
Languages: Spanish, with regional variations affecting both accent and vocabulary; African words restricted mainly to religious terms.
Religion: there is no established church. Some Cubans are Roman Catholic, there are many Protestant churches, and Afro-Cuban religions are very popular.

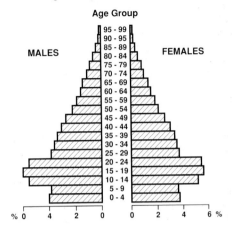

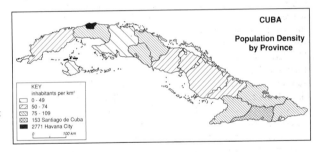

C

HISTORY AND POLITICS

Key historical dates: * c. 1000BC: Siboneys settle in Cuba, followed later by Taínos from Orinoco basin * 1492: Columbus sights Cuba and lands at Gibara on 28 October * 1511-14: Diego Velásquez and Pánfilo Narváez oversee the occupation of Cuba and the foundation of the colony's first towns * 1607: Havana replaces Santiago de Cuba as capital * 1762: the British occupy Havana for 10 months and break Spain's monopoly on trade * 1789: a royal decree authorises free trade in slaves * 1812: the Aponte uprising, the first major rebellion by slaves in Cuba * 1818: Spain opens Cuban ports to free international trade * 1837: the laying of Cuba's first railway (the first in Latin America) * 1848-51: Narciso López, former soldier in Spanish army, leads three failed invasions of Cuba, with aim of annexing the island to the US * 1868-78: the Ten Years' War in Oriente province fails to free Cuba of Spanish rule * 1878: in the 'Protest of Baraguá', Antonio Maceo denounces the Pact of Zanjón which ended the war and leaves the country * 1886: Spain abolishes slavery * 1892: José Martí founds the Cuban Revolutionary Party in Florida * 1895: the Cuban war of independence begins on 24 February * 1898: the US intervenes following the sinking of the *USS Maine* and in December signs the Treaty of Paris with Spain *

74

20.5.1902: Cuba is declared a Republic and US forces withdraw * 1903: Cuba adopts the Platt Amendment, allowing the Americans to intervene to 'defend' Cuban independence and granting them a naval base at Guantánamo * 1924: Gerardo Machado elected president, beginning of a harsh dictatorship * 1933: a general strike forces Machado out, and rebel sergeants under Fulgencio Batista take over * 1940: Batista wins the presidency but loses it four years later * 1952: Batista stages a coup, 'abolishes' the constitution and presides over ruthless military dictatorship * 23.7.1953: Fidel Castro leads an attack on the Moncada barracks in Santiago * May 1955: Fidel Castro is released and leaves for Mexico * 1956: Castro and 81 revolutionaries return to Cuba aboard the *Granma* yacht and launch guerrilla insurgency from the Sierra Maestra mountains * 1.1.1959: Fulgencio Batista flees Havana and the army surrenders * 1959: Castro's new government introduces agrarian reform and other radical changes * 1960: American assets are nationalised and Washington imposes trade embargo * April 1961: the Bay of Pigs invasion by US-backed Cuban exiles fails * October 1962: the Cuban Missile Crisis * 1965: Cuba's alliance of revolutionary parties reorganised as the Partido Comunista de Cuba (PCC) * 1967: Che Guevara killed in Bolivia * 1968: a 'revolutionary offensive' includes the nationalisation of all remaining small businesses * 1970: the attempt to produce a 10-million ton sugar harvest fails, prompting closer links with the USSR to avert economic crisis * 1975: first PCC congress convened * 1976: new constitution and assemblies of

People's Power approved * 1977: Washington and Havana re-establish limited diplomatic relations * 1978: Cuban exiles in Miami are allowed to return to Cuba for family visits * 1980: the Mariel boatlift results in the emigration of 125,000 Cubans to Miami * 1986: the Rectification of Errors ends brief experiment with private enterprise * 1988: an accord in New York brings the withdrawal of Cuban troops from Angola * 1989: trial and execution of General Ochoa heralds clampdown on those in favour of *perestroika*-style reform * 1990: the 'Special Period in Peace Time' introduces massive austerity measures to Cuba * 1991: 4th PCC Congress decides to admit Catholics into the party for the first time * 1992: Torricelli Bill, tightening up the US trade embargo, passed in Washington * 1993: depenalisation of the dollar and introduction of limited private enterprise * 5.8.1994: riot in Havana sparks the biggest exodus of boatpeople since Mariel.

Constitution: Cuba's socialist constitution states that 'all the power belongs to the working people and is exercised through the Assemblies of People's Power'. The *Asamblea Nacional de Poder Popular*, with 589 members (1993), is elected by the people every five years. The 30-member *Consejo de Estado* and the 44-member *Consejo de Ministros* are the two highest government bodies. *Head of State:* Fidel Castro Ruz, constitutional head of state since 2 December 1976, although *de facto* leader since 1959. Titles: President of the Council of State and Council of Ministers, Secretary-General of the Communist Party and Commander-in-Chief of the Revolutionary Armed Forces.

Political Parties: Partido Comunista de Cuba (PCC), the 'supreme leading force of society and state', is the only legal political party. *Armed forces (1991 Western estimates):* army 145,000 (including conscripts), navy 13,500, airforce 22,000; army reserves 135,000; State Security troops 120,000; border guards 4,000, EJT (youth army) 100,000; people's militia 1.3 million. *Membership of international organisations:* UN and UN organisations; Caribbean Tourism Association; Caribbean Trade Organisation; Association of Caribbean States. *Media and communications:* 343 radios, 203 television sets and 56.4 telephones per 1,000 inhabitants (UK/US: 1,146/2,123 radios, 435/ 815 television sets, 477/789 telephones). Newspapers (these figures are based on the late 1980s, since then shortages have drastically reduced newspaper output): since 1990 *Granma* (400,000 circulation; Cuban Communist Party) has been the only daily newspaper available; *Juventud Rebelde* (250,000; Unión de Jovenes Comunistas) and *Trabajadores* (150,000; CTC) are now only weekly; an international edition of *Granma* also appears weekly, in English, French, Spanish and Portuguese; 15 provincial papers appear weekly if at all. One of the most widely-read monthly journals is the cultural magazine, *Bohemia.* Cuba has 5 national radio stations and one international network (Radio Habana Cuba), in addition to about 50 local stations. There are 2 national television networks, Cubavisión and Tele-Rebelde, which broadcast only in the evenings except on Sundays.

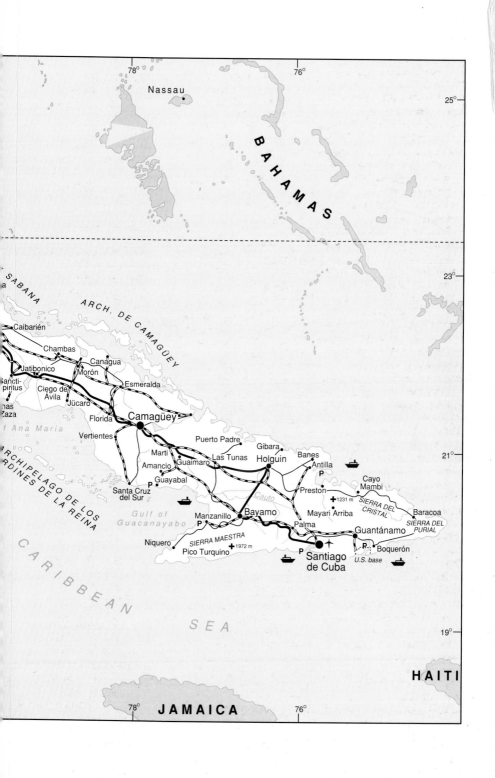